C000256540

The CatMan of Darby Road

Kamran Nayeri

THE CAT MAN OF DARBY ROAD

All text and photos copyright © 2022, Kamran Nayeri

All rights reserved. This book or any portion thereof may not be reproduced or used in any manner whatsoever without the express written permission of the publisher except for the use of brief quotations in a book review.

Print ISBN: 978-1-66783-1-114
eBook ISBN: 978-1-66783-1-121

To Mary Suzanne Sears, friend for 52 years,

who helped me learn English and to drive a car,

but most of all, for bringing Nuppy into my life

"This book is not about pets. It is not likely to be a comfortable reading for those who think that love for animals involves no more than stroking a cat or feeding birds in the garden. It is intended rather for people who are concerned about ending oppression and exploitation wherever they occur, and in seeing that the basic moral principle of equal consideration of interest is not arbitrarily restricted to members of our own species."

Peter Singer, *Animal Liberation*, 1975

CONTENTS

Acknowledgement

This book is a homage to 20 feral cats I have known and taken care of over a 20-year period. In these years, my life has been intertwined with theirs, two of them are still alive and live with me and enrich my life. The cats have been central to my life for their daily requirements but also for problems they faced, whether illness or dangers from predators, hazardous weather and other adverse conditions, or from human malice. As I will explain in the book, my interactions with these cats helped develop their personalities and they in turn helped to develop mine. I believe they have helped make me a better human being with a much wider view of life and humanity's place in the web of life. Thus, although they are the focus of the book, the book is also autobiographical, hence the title of the book.

I am also grateful to all who helped me in caring for these cats, especially doctors Jessica Baldwin, Patricia Alexander, Shannon Cloninger, and the staff of Analy Veterinary Hospital in Sebastopol California. Many thanks to my friends and neighbors Greg Storino and John Woodward who helped me with building cat condos and feeding stations for the feral cats on Darby Road.

I am grateful to the poet and writer Vanessa Jimenez Gabb who read the manuscript, encouraged me to publish it, and lightly edited it and to Mehdi Gooran Savadkoohi of Simorgh Graphic Design Studio, Tehran, Iran, who designed the cover of the book and Fahimeh Gooran, friend for 30 years, and a lifelong graphic designer, who facilitated and contributed to the process.

This book is written as creative nonfiction. Names of human individuals who appear in it are either used with their explicit permission or are names of professionals who provided care for the cats. Otherwise, I have used fictitious names.

Introduction

It is before dawn on Thanksgiving Day 2020. I awake laying on my back wrapped under a blanket as Siah, who had slept upstairs, jumps on the bed and walks over my legs to the left side of the bed. I stretch out my left arm as he slowly makes his way towards my head resting on the pillow. I feel his front left leg stretch out towards my left shoulder and then slightly crosses it. He then stretches out his entire body cuddling against mine as he rests his head in my armpit. Still half asleep, I take my right arm out of the covers and help him snuggle alongside my body. As I press him with my right hand against me, I raise my head and kiss his forehead, behind his ears, and his cheeks. His body relaxes as I press him against my body while covering him with the blanket. I hear him give out a sigh. He begins to purr. Soon he begins to breathe heavily, falling fast asleep, and so do I.

Somehow, Siah and I developed this routine which he initiates most predawn mornings. We both love snuggling together in the wee hours of the morning.

Siah is a seven year-old sixteen pound black male cat who was dumped in the neighborhood five years ago. For months he wandered around lost, scared, and hungry. Until he found La Casa de Los Gatos, a Tahoe-style house on two acres of land three miles outside of the town of Sebastopol that has a population of 8,000. It is amazing how two total strangers, he and I, became such close friends so quickly.

Panther, my other black male cat, does the same when Siah is sleeping upstairs in the loft. Except Panther has his own routine. He often sleeps curled up against me with his head towards the bottom of the bed. Panther sleeps much less than Siah and for that matter, most cats. So when he rests by me, he spends much time grooming his fine shiny coat. Like Siah, Panther was also dumped in the neighborhood and found me, and this house that he made his own, nine years ago.

For the last 20 years, my life and the life of 20 feral cats have merged as they have found me and I have found them. Part of this story unfolds when I lived in a house on Chelton Drive, Montclair, Oakland from 1998 to 2001. The second part of the story is about feral cats on Darby Road, a country road outside of the small town of Sebastopol, California. This part of the story covers 2011-2018. While in Oakland the cats came to the house where I lived either to live inside or to live around the house, the feral cats on Darby Road already had their own "home" when I met them. This required me to drive to where they lived twice daily to serve their meals and socialize with them. During this seven-year period, I could not take a single day off from my duties to these cats. I could not find anyone who would help me even when I attempted to hire someone for a short duration so I could go on a brief vacation.

This intensive interaction with so many cats over a two-decade long period helped me observe how each cat was transformed as she or he bonded with me. Some even became a house cat due to circumstances. Others remained feral but allowed me into their lives to various degrees. If I helped change these cats lives, they in turn transformed me and my life. They taught me about the world of cats, and through it, they taught me about the world of us humans. I hope to show in this book how such transformations unfolded and some of the insight I gained through getting to know these cats. In this book I will tell the stories of these cats in some detail except for the few who I knew for very brief period of time as they were too sick and had to be euthanized or they simply went away to die in isolation.

As I am a hobbyist nature and wildlife photographer, I have taken photos of most of the cats detailed in this book. Some of these as well as photos of the houses where I and some of these cats lived in this 20-year period are provided in the *Photo Gallery* at the end of the book.

Because life events impact us crucially, depending on our earlier experiences and our personal make up, a few words about myself are in order. I was born in Tehran, Iran, in 1950 and lived there until 1969 when I came to the United States to go to college and eventually decided to live here. Since childhood, I have been revolted by all manners of brutality against non-human animals (of course, we, humans, are animals ourselves; we just don't like to acknowledge it). In Tehran, I saw feral cats when they climbed the walls of our house in search of food (as houses in Iran are walled). My mother sometimes gave these cats leftovers or residues of meat, chicken, or fish she used in cooking. When I was a teenager she actually named a feral cat and treated her as her own although the cat did not live in the house. Still, my parents were decidedly against feral cats. On more than one occasion, my father bagged the cat and took her miles away and released her. In one case, to their amazement, the cat returned and my mother felt obligated to feed her as her own.

In my preschool age, my parents adopted a midsize female dog whom they named Fidel. Fidel was chained during the day in what was supposed to have been a garage but was too short to allow in even a Volkswagen Beetle and was let loose to run inside the yard at night. In other words, she was serving as a watchdog.

I loved Fidel and my uncle's German shepherd who was named Black. My uncle lived a short walking distance away from us so Black visited Fidel frequently. They loved playing together.

There were many feral dogs in Narmak, the newly established district in the northeastern outskirts of Tehran in the 1950s where we lived. Unbeknown to us, the municipality decided to get rid of the feral dogs by poisoning them. One day we found Fidel dead after being poisoned by the municipality workers. I became familiar with the plight of feral dogs.

In 1950s Iran, many services were still provided by artisans and peddlers who carried their wares or merchandise on the backs of donkeys. Donkeys were also used for carrying heavy loads from wholesale to retail shops. I saw donkeys struggling under heavy weight whom were beaten by a stick to carry on. Some even had sores on their backs and necks.

In the early 1960s, our family spent three years in <u>Borazjan</u>, a town of 15,000 at the time, near the Persian Gulf. We arrived there in the midst of a seven-year drought. Everyone suffered, especially farm animals. I saw a horse, skin and bones, being sold in the market for a quarter as the farmer could not feed him. Kids in my neighborhood poured gasoline in snake holes and set them on fire for fun. Feral cats were set on fire and at night boys ganged up on feral dogs who ventured into the alleyways at night in search of food and beat them up with stones and sticks. Two of my father's friends were deer hunters and would go at night when they could blind the deer with the headlights and shoot them at close range. One morning they stopped by our house with the bloody corpse of a deer tied up to the front of the jeep to give my mother a cut. It made me sick in the stomach. My mother, on the other hand, was glad to make kabob out of the deer meat. As long as she lived, whenever I admiringly pointed out deer grazing in the distance with their fawns she rejoiced: "they made good kabob."

There is no consensus about the number of cats in the world. But all estimates are in the hundred of millions. Most of these cats that are feral are defined as domesticated cats that are homeless and, to a varying degree, untamed. However, even the definition of domestication is murky. Feral cats can manage to live on their own and reproduce but often with much difficulty and many live miserable short lives. It is well established that domestication alters both the domesticated and the domesticator in many ways. In my own experience taking care of feral cats has made me bond with other species as well.

Kamran Nayeri

Sebastopol, California, January 2022

The Cats at Chelton Drive, Oakland

I easily fall in love with cats.

But falling in love with cats is a learned behavior. In fact, for the first 49 years of my life I was largely blind to the presence of cats. I retained my blind spot for cats even when my mother took care of a few feral cats over the years and after falling in love with a woman in college who loved and had cats. When, in April 1975, when got married, she cared for a black female cat named Shark. I regret that I never really bonded with Shark. In 1999 all this changed because of a cat named Nuppy.

I lived in Brooklyn, New York, for seventeen years before I relocated to Oakland, California in 1997. In December 1997 I moved into a house on Chelton Drive in the Montclair neighborhood of Oakland. Montclair is located along the western slope of the Oakland Hills from a valley formed by the Hayward Fault to the upper ridge of the hills. It also borders the Redwood Regional Park with a large network of hiking trails. Dotted with homes pinned on hillsides connected to highway 13 by a network of narrow winding streets, Montclair is a quiet neighborhood with easy access to downtown Oakland and San Francisco.

The house had two bedrooms and two full baths and a study on the bottom floor. I remodeled the top floor to be one very large room with the kitchen on the south end and the sitting room on the northern side. The center was made into the dining area with a large table and eight chairs.

The two floors were connected by a stairway on the east side and there was a narrow balcony on each floor made of redwood facing the valley on the west side. There were two exit doors. The front door was on the top floor that opened to a set of 15 steps that reached to Chelton Drive. There was a driveway leading to a two-car garage on the top of the house. The second door to the outside opened to the space below the driveway and was a quick way to get to the western side of the house with a door that led to the crawl space which housed the water heater and the furnace.

1. Nuppy

In Spring of 1999, Mary arrived from New York with two cats in what turned out to be our last failed attempt to rekindle a romantic relationship we once enjoyed in college. Thus, we remained, as always, friends, and once again, housemates.

Soon after Mary arrived, her older cat, Seaweed, who suffered from late-stage chronic kidney disease, died. The young and strong, seven-year old cat, Nuppy, took over the whole house. A white alpha male with blond patches on his head, back and sides, Nuppy was known to be a menace to other cats and he even attacked people. When I lived in New York and visited Mary's apartment in the East Village in the mid-1990s, she forewarned me about him. Mary had cordoned off the railroad apartment to keep Seaweed in the bedroom facing Tompkins Square Park and Nuppy in the bathroom and closet area in the opposite end. Mary explained to me how Nuppy spent a lot of time trying to break out to attack Seaweed with occasional success. Likewise, given the opportunity, Nuppy would attack visitors. Once, he jumped on the sofa in the hallway to bite my arm.

At the time, I had no clue about cat behavior and none of this made me like Nuppy. I sympathized with Seaweed, an older female cat, whose home was invaded by this young, strong, and brutish male cat.

In my own mind, I also partly blamed Mary for creating this ongoing conflict in her small apartment. Of course, she had explained the circumstances of her adoption of Nuppy. On a visit to her aging parents in Bellaire, a small town situated inside Houston, in 1992, Mary's father found Nuppy as a kitten still with closed eyes in the toolshed. Apparently, Nuppy's mother, a feral cat, had given birth there and for some reason, soon afterwards she relocated her kittens to the basement of the neighbor. Somehow, she did not take Nuppy.

Mary nursed Nuppy while visiting her parents. Given her parents' infirmity, Mary decided to take Nuppy to New York. Nuppy was lucky. Mary later learned the neighbor had killed Nuppy's mother and siblings. When Mary told me this story I was shaken up.

In the early days of his arrival, Nuppy attacked my bare ankle a number of times. It was always a surprise attack. The last time Nuppy tried another attack we were both in the living room at the top floor of the house. I took my rubber slipper off and threw it at him as I let out a screaming "NO!" The slipper hit him in the back as he tried to run down the stairs to the bottom floor where the bedrooms were. He paused for a moment to look at me and then disappeared in the stairwell.

Somehow that experience changed Nuppy's behavior towards me. The surprise attacks stopped. He mellowed out and directed his aggressive energy towards the toys we bought for him. He gradually began to scent mark me by rubbing his chin against my legs or my hands. I began to return the favor by caressing his head, behind the ears, and back. He purred as a sign of pleasure and approval. I began to hold him in my arms and kiss his forehead.

We both liked the change!

As Nuppy and I became friends he opened up a new understanding of cats in me. When Mary and I were planning for her relocation to Oakland she assured me that the cats would not be messy and promised to put their litter box outside the house to avoid odor. Of course, she knew that would not be practical but it gave me a short period to adjust. As Nuppy and I became friends, the litter box was placed in my study!

Initially, Nuppy slept in Mary's bedroom on the east side of the house. Over time, he began splitting his time between her bedroom and mine on the west side. Within a couple of years, he slept most nights next to me. I slept better with him next to me!

Nuppy's bonding with me even included an odd behavior. I took my shower each night before bed time. After the shower, I put on my two-piece pajamas and walked into the bedroom to rest, read, and eventually go to sleep. Nuppy began to attack the cuff of my pajama pants holding onto it with his fangs. I was forced to take them off. He would then hold it in his mouth while doing a nursing dance as kittens do when sucking milk from their mother's nipple. However, there was a sexual undertone to this ritual as his pinky was also exposed. Mary and I treated this as an amusing behavior letting him have his fun with my pajama. We even made him a song which we sang when he was busy doing his routine: "Humpy, humpy, humpy boy, Nuppy is such a humpy boy!" After doing his dance until he got tired , Nuppy would join me in the bed for a good night of sleep.

While Nuppy clearly loved me and spent a lot of time with me, Mary remained his "mamma." Mary and I joked that I was "not the mamma" after the animation series "Dinosaurs" in which the baby dinosaur called his father "not the mamma!"

Nuppy turned out to be quite a social cat. When we had dinner parties, we always set a bed for him on a seat next to ours. He enjoyed sitting there, watching us eat, drink, and socialize with friends. When we did our Sunday yoga taught by our friend Simin, and attended by my colleagues and friends Jim and Mona, Nuppy liked to sit on the warm air vent and watch us do the routine.

Meanwhile, Nuppy's habit of biting me had turned into gentle love bites on my hands or fingers. Over the years, I have learned that alpha cats sometimes display dominance by biting other cats and also humans they actually take as their friends. At first, it is not a well-calibrated bite and will hurt and can even draw blood. But as the cat and his object of domination both realize it is just a game, the bite becomes gentle and playful. Over time, the bite becomes a lick as the object of domination becomes part of the domineering cat's sense of self.

Being raised on the fifth floor of a brownstone in the East Village in Manhattan, Nuppy had never learned to be outside and deal with its dangers. The front door of the house opened to Chelton Drive via 15 redwood steps. The driveway was like a bridge from the street to the garage with trash and recycling bins were on the side farther from the front steps and we had some plants on the side by the stairway. While Chelton Drive was not a busy street and occasional cars drove at a slow speed due to the narrowness and winding layout of the street, we were concerned with Nuppy's safety. Being a cat, Nuppy was curious about what was going on on the driveway and in the street, especially as people, some with dogs, and neighbors' cats, went by.

On my insistence, Mary agreed to allow Nuppy out on the top step by the street behind a fence that we erected. There he could watch the street and what passed by without being able to venture into the street or driveway and beyond. Nuppy obviously enjoyed this much wider world. After he was acclimated to the outdoors somewhat, he broke out a few times. Each time, we took him back inside as he was under close supervision.

But gradually we felt comfortable with Nuppy going out and coming back in on his own.

We also had to manage Nuppy not to get into fights with other cats in the neighborhood. We knew of two: Simon, who lived with our next door neighbors Anne and Tony. And Bogie, a tuxedo cat, that was taken care of by our neighbors across the street, Betty and Sam. Both cats were male. But they were of two very different personalities. Simon was afraid of and ran away from bigger cats but attacked smaller more vulnerable cats. Mary and I talked about his "character flaw." Bogie on the other hand was unusual in his dealings with other cats. He walked deliberately and with confidence but not in any way threatening past other cats. Somehow, he managed not to get into fights with them. We called him the "cool cat."

Even Nuppy couldn't start a fight with Bogie, who simply ignored his threatening gestures.

In 2006, two other cats found their way to our house. One day when I was serving food to Bogie near the driveway, I noticed a tabby orange cat atop the cement retaining wall across the street behind the garbage bins our neighbors had put out for the weekly pick-up service. The cat was obviously malnourished and hungry. I took a dish of food and slowly walked to the retaining wall as the cat retreated into the bushes in the background. I left the dish there and walked back. The cat returned quickly and ate all the food in a hurry. I served him more food and he ate more until he had eaten enough and left.

From then on, the tabby orange cat returned when I was serving food to Bogie on the driveway. In the years that followed, I learned that feral cats, as well as wildlife in our neighborhood, keep us under close watch before they make the decision to reveal themselves to us. They know a lot more about us than we know about them when we meet.

I served Bogie and George, the name Mary gave the orange tabby cat who we knew was male because he was not neutered, at the same time. In due time, George found himself a spot in our other next door neighbor's crawl space which provided some dry spot less exposed to the elements in winter time. It became our task to avoid a fight between Nuppy and George as both cats were male and neither would back away from a fight. Once, to diffuse hostility, I had to rush in to snatch Nuppy as he was about to charge George.

In November 2006, I moved from working at University of California Data Archive and Technical Assistance/Survey Research Center at UC Berkeley to the University of California Office of the President in downtown Oakland. For the previous three years, I had been taking care of a feral cat there. Mooshi, as I named her, was a beautiful young female calico cat. I had to take her home. I will return to the story of Mooshi soon. But when

I took Mooshi home it proved very difficult to keep Nuppy from attacking her. At first, we had to keep Mooshi in Mary's bedroom and close the door to Nuppy. Later, when Mooshi had gotten somewhat used to being at her new home, we partitioned the lower floor to give her more room which included Mary's bedroom, bathroom and my study. Nuppy had my bedroom and the entire top floor. Mary, who worked from home until 2004, now had a 9-5 office job. So, Nuppy and Mooshi were home alone!

Towards the end of his life, Nuppy calmed down a little. Mooshi was able to explore the entire house while we watched over Nuppy. For instance, when we had dinner, we placed Nuppy's bed on the dining table while Mooshi rested on a cushion on the wooden bench near the fireplace. Every few minutes Nuppy would try to sneak away to charge Mooshi. We had to distract him. To her credit, Mooshi, who was a fighter, did not back down or hide. She took territory as it was made available under our protection.

Nuppy was a healthy and happy cat. But he also suffered at times in part because of our ignorance. Mary had a claw-clipper and every once in a while I had to hold Nuppy in my arm as she clipped the tip of his claws. Both of us have never tried to clip any other cat since. Sometimes, our ignorance caused far more damage to Nuppy.

One day, I came home and found him just inside the living room from the open sliding door to the balcony laying on his side with a bloody mouth. I looked around for a clue as to what might have happened and found a clay plant pot lying on its side on the platform of the redwood balcony. My worst fears had come to pass. Mary had lined up clay plant pots on top of the railing of the balcony, despite my objection. I had expressed my fear that the wind or some other force could cause the pots to fall on Nuppy who loved to bask in the sun on the balcony.

I quickly placed Nuppy inside a carrier and drove as fast as I could to the Albany VCA Animal Hospital. They immediately took him in for emergency surgery, sewing up his jaw that was broken. It took Nuppy weeks to fully recuperate.

In late 2007, Nuppy began defecating on the carpet in my bedroom. When we took him to the Albany VCA Animal Hospital, it was found that he suffered from late-stage chronic kidney disease. While Mary had cats for many years, she and I were uneducated about cat's health and veterinary science at the time was less developed. There were two contributing factors to Nuppy's chronic kidney disease. Since his early days, Mary offered water to Nuppy through a needleless syringe. Later, she trained him to drink from her finger held under a running faucet. Thus, Nuppy would not drink water from a bowl or not at least as much as a regular cat would. Nuppy was also on dried cat food. Thus, he was probably chronically dehydrated.

His veterinarian recommended rehydration with electrolyte injection solution. Nuppy was very averse to trips to the hospital and being handled by strangers. So we tried to do the injections at home. Mary took charge of administering the needle while I kept Nuppy still. After a few times trying, we decided that Nuppy was miserable being held down and a big long needle being inserted into his back and being kept still for the duration of the drip. And we could not do a good job. The procedure would have given Nuppy a few weeks or a few months of extended life. We decided to let the disease take its course.

Within a short period, I found Nuppy hiding in the closet. Very sick cats self-isolate. We took Nuppy to the VCA and they recommended keeping him overnight to rehydrate him. Nuppy spent three nights there. We knew Nuppy was miserable being kept in a cage for that long and handled by strangers who poked him with a big needle. But what was the alternative? After the third night, they called us to take Nuppy home. I brought Nuppy home after work and he immediately went into the closet in my bedroom and looked terribly ill. As the night progressed Nuppy seemed increasingly more miserable. I suggested to Mary, and she accepted, to put Nuppy out of his misery.

I picked up Nuppy, who put up a minor resistance, and placed him in the carrier. I still blame myself for forcing him as I had come to honor his wishes. With Mary, I drove to a 24-hour cat and dog hospital on University Avenue in Berkeley. A young veterinarian was at work. I explained the situation and asked her to euthanize Nuppy. She asked if either one of us wanted to be present. Neither Mary nor I could stomach it. She took Nuppy to the back without us even giving him a goodbye hug or a kiss. At exactly midnight she returned with the carrier. Nuppy's dead body wrapped in a blanket was inside. He felt more heavy than usual.

For the duration of our trip back home Mary and I did not exchange a word. We left Nuppy's body inside the carrier on the balcony as it was a warm night.

The next morning we dug a hole in the rocky grounds behind the house and placed Nuppy wrapped in his blanket inside the hole. As I was pouring soil on his dead body, I suddenly broke down, tears running down my face, my body shaking uncontrollably. I had never lost anyone I loved as much as Nuppy. Mary had to finish the job of covering his grave.

My best friend had gone beyond my reach. I had never felt so defeated in my life before.

In a space of nine years, Nuppy had become someone that I loved the most in all of my life. Often people took this as an insult to my close relatives and friends. But Nuppy had taught me a key lesson these people had not learned: *a cat is a person*. Nuppy became my friend on par with some of my best human friends. My human friends who I hold dear to my heart have taken a different path in life and our friendship has grown weak or simply withered away. Not so with Nuppy or with any other cat I came to know in the twenty years since Nuppy came into my life.

The love Nuppy gave me was unconditional love. The only other such love I ever had in my life was from my mother, a maternal love.

11. Bogie

Bogie was an amazing cat. A great hunter, he was also able to coexist with other cats and avoid fights. A tuxedo male cat, he walked a cool walk, swinging his body gently and slightly to the right and to the left as he moved straight ahead but always flexible enough to walk past a challenger pacifying him. Thus, I never saw him in a fight with Nuppy. Mary likes to think that Bogie's cool manners helped him to live a long life that she estimated to be about 21 years.

What we knew about Bogie's early years came from Betty and Sam who lived there long before I arrived. Apparently, a young man who was a drummer and lived with our neighbors to the South, Anne and Tony, adopted Bogie as a kitten from someone in front of Safeway in Montclair Village sometime in 1994. Within a few years, the young man decided to move and as he loaded his car with his belongings, Bogie found an opportunity to jump out of the car and ran into the bushes. Apparently, Bogie was fed up with all the drumming (and who can blame him for that!). The young man did not make an effort to find Bogie and took off. Thus, Bogie became a feral cat hunting rodents to survive. Sometime later, Bogie began to visit Betty and Sam's house across the road and getting occasional meals from them.

Soon after Mary arrived in 1999, she got to know Miles, a Jack Russell Terrier, who sometimes came down to the house and barked at me, and made friends with Betty. As she worked part time from home on her programming job in New York, Mary befriended Betty and had tea-time visits. She then began to walk Miles every day. Betty was obese with chronic health issues and Sam was working long days. Soon, Mary became friends also with Ralph, a Shih Tzu, the other dog at their house. In those visits she got to meet Bogie.

A couple of years later, Sam retired and the couple decided to move to Washington State. They left Bogie behind and did not tell Mary about it. Some three months later, one day Mary spotted Bogie on the hillside by Anne and Tony's house. She called out to him and Bogie came and ate. Bogie had lost weight for lack of a regular meal.

From then on Bogie stopped by the driveway and was served his meals and Mary gave him love and attention. Clearly, Bogie was ready to come into the house but that was not possible because of Nuppy. We already had Mooshi in the house and were trying to deal with Nuppy's aggression towards her.

It was winter and biting cold in Montclair. So, we put a cat door on the lower right corner of the garage door and Bogie learned to come in and go out as he pleased. To acclimate him to his spot inside the garage, initially either Mary or I would take him inside in the evening and close the garage door. There we sat on a chair with him on our lap to comfort him sufficiently to get him relaxed and sleepy and then place him in his bed and leave, closing the garage door. Bogie learned the routine and stayed in his bed. It was still damn cold in the garage as the roof and sidings had no insulation, but it was still a notch better than being outside exposed to the elements. Later, when we tried to get George to sleep in the garage, we insulated it.

After Nuppy's death on May 15, 2008, Bogie came into the house. We made a cat door in the door that opened to the retaining wall under the driveway for Bogie to come and go as he pleased. Of course, raccoons also learned about the cat door and we had to make sure to lock it from the inside and let Bogie in when he showed up late at night.

One year, a mother raccoon, who we named Rocky, began to show up with her four baby raccoons to eat leftover cat food. Rocky arrived either by the lower floor door or on the steps to the front door. We would give her and her babies leftover cat food and back away. It was wonderful watching them eat with their hands and then wash them in the water bowel we also provided. After that experience, we routinely placed leftover cat food on the tree stump on the side of the hill away from the street.

Bogie slept in Mary's bedroom as Mooshi slept in my bed usually between or over my legs. Over time, Bogie also began to sleep in my bed but he slept close to my head, curled up next to me.

In August 2011, I left Montclair to live in a house on two acres outside of Sebastopol, Sonoma County, part of the famed California wine country. I took Mooshi with me, Bogie, who was part of the neighborhood even before I arrived there, and Fluffy, the feral female tabby orange cat who suddenly showed up near Anne and Tony's house in the summer of 2008 and who we brought inside the house stayed with Mary.

Bogie lived a happy cat as he loved Mary and she loved him tremendously. In the last couple of years of his long life, Bogie slowed down. He died in Mary's arms on February 26, 2015. Mary attributes his death to "old age." He was in Mary's estimate about 21 years old.

III. George

George left us as he arrived, almost as if it was his choice. And on a certain level, it perhaps was.

Sometimes in fall of 2005 when I was serving food to Bogie, I noticed a tabby orange cat sitting atop the cement retaining wall across the street. He looked malnourished and hungry. I served him food.

I did not see him for some time after that day. But he showed up again and I fed him again. He began to more frequently visit us and increasingly trusted us. Mary named him George. We could tell his gender because he was not neutered. George was in a bad shape. He suffered from malnutrition, his left forearm hurt as he kept it up when he sat down, his right ear folding forward. He had these sad big round eyes. He was very wary of people; we never managed to touch him.

At first, Bogie, but especially Nuppy, tried to keep George away. But eventually, George joined the group of cats at and around our house. He quickly learned the breakfast and dinner schedule and during the day went inside the garage through the cat door for snacks or water.

Over time, George's health improved. His fur became healthier, his forearm healed, and his ear straightened out. A few times, I saw George following a younger cat up the hill among the bushes. The younger cat looked like George. Mary and I thought it may be George's offspring. This cat also showed up from time to time to eat the food in the garage, but she looked healthy and I think she might have had someone that fed her more or less daily.

From time to time, George did not show up for his meals or the dry food in the garage would remain untouched. I thought he might have found food elsewhere. But he would show up somewhat worn out. But things would return to normal and he would eat with a good appetite. Being an older cat, I was worried if he would survive the winter. Just before winter, we insulated the garage and made a couple of nice beddings for George. Soon after that, George began to sleep in the garage. We felt good about this.

What is more, George began coming into the house to eat and to venture. At one point, he sprayed the house to mark it as his territory.

What we did not know was that George was suffering from a serious disease. Beginning in January, George became increasingly finicky. First, he did not like his salmon wet food anymore. We tried to offer other flavors. Gradually, he stopped eating most of the food that he really liked. When he ate, he did so with difficulty. He would eat only the top of his chunk of wet food. And he increasingly preferred liquids (but not water). So, we got him CatSure and lactose-free milk. He began to lose weight.

We found ourselves helpless. There was nothing reliable on the Internet to give us some clue of what to do to help George. I called the Montclair Veterinary Hospital to see if I could talk to a veterinarian for help. Dr. Richter called the following day. But he said he could not really offer much help without seeing the cat—which we could not arrange. We could not touch him and in the past trying to trap him was futile.

Finally, we borrowed a trap from a neighbor and within half an hour after setting it up George walked into it, no doubt due his confused state of mind.

Montclair Veterinary Hospital gave us an urgent care visit with a minimum of $600 charge. They took in George without giving us a chance to talk to the doctor and ran a series of tests. When all was done, Dr. Kim Smith came to the waiting room to discuss the result of her exam. "Everything seems more or less normal about George," she said. His blood work ruled out all infectious diseases, kidney disease, and almost everything else that could explain his condition. One of his kidneys had enlarged, so she wanted to take an X-Ray to consider the possibility of cancer. The result showed a well-formed but enlarged kidney. She did not think it looked cancerous. So, I asked her what could explain his condition. She did not offer any ideas. They had given him an antibiotic shot, something to stimulate his appetite and they gave us some prescription cat food that was supposed to be tasty and nutritious. Dr. Smith told us that the X-Ray showed a pellet in George's body. The bill was just shy of $800.

We went home, happy that George would pull out of this—after all, the doctor did not find anything wrong. We left George in the garage, left the door to his carrier open and closed the garage door. He immediately ran to the cat door and was trying hard to open it to leave the garage. We left him there for a while and after about 30 minutes, Mary opened the cat door so he could leave if he wanted. George left the garage and we did not see him again until a few days later.

On Thursday morning, when Mary opened the house door at 6 a.m, George was outside, half his former size hungry and thirsty. His eyes were sick and small. He came in and ate about a fourth of a can and drank some milk. He then went upstairs to sleep in the garage. It was a rainy and damp day.

Friday morning, I went to visit George in the garage. I also cleaned a litter box for him so he did not have to leave the garage for anything if he did not want to. It was a nice day. By mid-afternoon, it was about 59 degrees. When I went to the door to feed Fluffy, the female tabby orange cat, I found George in the box fitted with the towels we left by the door, a very small cat with sick small eyes. He put his head on his front paws resting. I offered him food and milk—he smelled them but did not take any. He then went back upstairs to the garage. He repeated this twice. The third time, he did not go to the garage. Instead, he sat on the top step like he had done many times in the past to enjoy the fresh air. He then lay down, his body thin as a sheet of paper.

At that moment, somehow it occurred to me that I might never see George again. I ran downstairs to get my camera to have a photo of him. When I came back up Bogie was standing above George, looking at him and smelling him, a very unusual situation. I called Bogie not to bother George and aimed to shoot a picture. Then came the mail truck—Bogie ran away, George dragged his body to the driveway and laid flat on his side in front of the garage. A little later, he went inside to rest.

George was a dignified cat—even when he came to us starving and badly hurt and sick or when he was dying. He liked to stretch by putting his forearms on the stairs and lowering his bottom. The day before we took him to the vet, George sat on the top stair while I sat a step below him. We locked our eyes together. He looked deeply into mine. As I look into his round sad eyes, tears rolled down my cheeks. I knew that my friend would not be with me for long. He got up and walked towards the garage, stopping at eye level, looking at me one more time. He then disappeared into the garage door.

The next morning, George was gone. We never saw him again.

IV. Fluffy

Sometime in the fall of 2007, we noticed a fluffy orange cat that ate the scraps of cat food we left for raccoons. While very skittish at first and afraid of Mooshi, Fluffy, as we called her, gradually joined George and Bogie to eat on the driveway. It did not take long before Fluffy felt comfortable enough to be hand fed with a fork by Mary. For some reason, Fluffy had no canine or incisor teeth. So it was unclear how she could have survived on her own. When we first saw Fluffy, Mary and I somehow believed she was George's daughter. They seemed to comfortably hang out together. Sometimes they greeted each other by smelling each other's faces, as if kissing each other on the cheek. If there was one dish of food, George let Fluffy eat first. Fluffy joined George to sleep in the crawl space of our neighbor's house.

Unlike George, Fluffy shed her fears of us quickly. Perhaps because of her unusual teeth, she actually liked eating wet food from a fork. So Mary and Fluffy had a daily arrangement to meet on the front door stairs for a meal Mary served to her. Gradually, Fluffy began to show up by the door under the driveway and sat on the railing to be fed. She felt comfortable enough to be brushed and fed at the same time. And this girl needed to be brushed daily! One day on an earlier agreement, as Mary was fork-feeding Fluffy, I picked her up and placed her inside the house in the stairway as Mary closed the door. Of course, Fluffy was confused for a short time not realizing where she was. But when she learned she was inside the house she went and hid under a bed. It took a while for her to get used to her new situation. But she already knew Mooshi and Bogie and there was no hostility between them. Fluffy became a house cat!

Fluffy remained shy of people for the rest of her life, but she felt at ease and preferred to be at home.

After Mooshi and I left in August of 2011 to live in La Casa de Los Gatos outside of Sebastopol, I did not see Fluffy much any more. On rare occasions when I visited, she was hiding from me as a stranger. But Fluffy felt comfortable with Mary and liked being brushed daily as her heavy coat matted quickly. Like Bogie who was in his really advanced age, Fluffy preferred staying home.

Fluffy's demise came suddenly. While Mary was away on her annual Christmas visit to her sister's house in Atlanta, the person who was taking care of Fluffy had to take her for an emergency visit to the veterinarian hospital in Montclair. She was diagnosed with advanced cancer and deemed eligible for euthanasia. She was euthanized on Dec. 23, 2016.

V. Mooshi

Of all the cats I have known, I knew Mooshi for the lon-gest period of time. Therefore, she was one of a few who was closest to my heart. If Nuppy was my friend, Mooshi was my "little girl," my daughter. What follows is my eulogy written after her death

> *"Thus shall ye think of all this fleeting world:*
> *"A star at dawn, a bubble in a stream,*
> *"A flash of lightning in a summer cloud,*
> *"A flickering lamp, a phantom, and a dream."*
> —Diamond Sutra, ca. fourth century CE

My Mooshi was euthanized on Friday, November 4, 2016. She took her last breath at about 10:25 a.m. It was a warm sunny morning, the kind she would have loved, sitting in her favorite spot in the garden between the miscanthus grass and the deer grass.

The process was relatively anxiety free for Mooshi. As with each veterinarian visit, she laid on the examination table. Leaning over, I held her in my arms to hug, kiss and comfort her (and to comfort me). She ate one or two pieces of cat treats from my hand. She was then given an injection of a sedative under the skin of her upper back. Within minutes she became sleepy. Then the fur from her back leg was shaved off to expose a vein and some sedative was rubbed on the exposed vein to make it numb. Finally, she was injected in the exposed vein with a dose of a drug that stopped her heart in a few seconds. I saw all this through a wall of tears as I was sobbing and holding onto her as if for eternity. I felt no sign of unease from Mooshi. She said nothing and did not move. When I was tapped on the shoulder I raised my head to look at Mooshi who was still lying there with her eyes half open. For a moment I thought she was still alive. Alas, her life-force was gone. There was her beautiful body, those green eyes, colorful fur, gorgeous face, lifeless. I realized that my Mooshi was gone forever. That I must carry on, without her beautiful presence, with the rest of my life.

I buried Mooshi under the redwood trees next to where I had laid Lulu to rest on February 13. When I placed her body inside her burial site and picked up some soil to spread on it, I smelled the earth, which reminded me of the scent of Mooshi's coat that I always adored.

Life and death have puzzled humanity for tens of thousands of years. Each of us confronts them according to our own understanding. Mine is rooted in science that understands life as an "emergent property", requiring energy flows to sustain and thrive. In this view, death is the negation of life, when an organism loses its ability to generate or process this vital energy flow. After death, organisms disintegrate into their constituent elementary chemical compounds. These, in turn, may become parts of a new living organism or energy flows that are necessary for sustaining them. In this sense, it is true that part of us may become part of one or more living organisms. However, this recycling of matter and energy is neither a "grand design" nor a non-material "soul" apart from the emergent property giving life to an organism. None of this denies the *magic of life* and the intrinsic value of each individual being. To the contrary: imagine the complexity of the conditions that have been necessary for the emergence of the first living organisms on Earth 3.8 billion years ago and for the emergence of more complex forms of life since.

There has never been and there will never be another Mooshi. Just like any other being, she was the product of her unique circumstances. Mooshi was probably born in 2000 near the Anna Head Buildings of the University of California, Berkeley, between Channing Way and Haste, somewhere in the block north of Telegraph Avenue. Legend has it that she was part of a litter and that her mother and siblings all perished soon after her birth. The campus Animal Control trapped, spayed and released Mooshi back into the same location. If this story is true it may explain Mooshi's feisty personality. It took me her lifetime to be able to secure enough of her trust to pick her up and hold her in my arms. And this was made possible in part due to Mooshi's increasing dependence on me for her daily functions as she became practically paralyzed in her back legs in the last year of her life.

If the reported account of her birth date is correct, Mooshi lived about sixteen years. She spent her life in almost equal parts in three locations. From 2000 to 2006, she lived as a feral cat in various spots under the Anna Head buildings where I worked and met her. When I had to move to a new job at the University of California Office of the President in Oakland, I worked with great difficulty to trap Mooshi and took her to my home on Chelton Drive in Montclair neighborhood of Oakland. She lived there from March 7, 2006 to August 20, 2011. Mooshi lived at her new residence on Darby Road, outside of Sebastopol, until her demise on November 4, 2016.

Mooshi got her name because one morning when I had first met her at the Survey Research Center's parking lot, I saw a disappearing mouse tail in her mouth. "Moosh" is "mouse" in Farsi and Mooshi denotes a mouser. Mooshi was bursting with energy those days. She enjoyed climbing all kinds of structures, including the metal mesh fence separating the parking lot from a childcare center and even the three-story high Anna Head building itself which she climbed to the top (giving me a minor heart attack in the process). She was very smart. In cold winter mornings in Berkeley, she sat on the hood of the most recently-arrived car to warm up. Being raised in a parking lot made her car and people smart. She was not afraid of them but she was wary of them getting too close. Most evenings she sat on the balcony of the Survey Research Center building observing office workers leaving for home in their cars. To me it was a heartbreak each evening to leave Mooshi behind. Each evening I asked her: "Would you like to go home with me?" Because of Mooshi, I went to work seven days a week, even on Christmas, to ensure she ate well and had company.

About six months before I moved to my new job in downtown Oakland, I began plotting to trap Mooshi. I never trapped anyone and hated the idea of doing it. I had a number of false starts. One was to enlist the husband of a coworker who claimed to be a cat whisperer. He came and left a worn-out jacket near where I placed Mooshi's water and food dishes. The idea was that Mooshi would become familiar with his smell and he then could get close enough to scoop her up and put her in a bag for me to take home. He could not even get close to Mooshi. Finally, I enlisted the help of a very kind and helpful woman who worked for the campus Animal Control. She suggested using a cone-shaped net with a pool-sized handle to trap Moohi from behind as she ate. Mooshi was far too smart to allow me pull off a trick like that! When all else failed, the same kind woman provided me with a raccoon trap. She told me to stop feeding Mooshi and to set up the trap each morning with smelly food like tuna and sardine inside. It took eight heart-wrenching days for Mooshi to finally cave in to hunger and walk into the trap. I quickly took Mooshi to the Albany VCA Animal Hospital on Solano Avenue. She was examined and had no infections. But some of her teeth were broken and had to be pulled. The veterinarian told me that she might have become very sick and died of infection in her mouth if I had not brought her in.

When we got home, Mary had prepared her bathroom for Mooshi's arrival. While she was still heavily sedated, I placed Mooshi inside the bathtub, which was covered with a blanket and several towels to make it soft and comfortable. We left her drinking water and a litter box. Food was out of the question until her gums healed.

Mooshi pulled through and began eating. At that point, Mary and I temporarily exchanged bedrooms so I could sleep with Mooshi, who quickly found refuge under Mary's bed. For almost a week, Mooshi tried to crash the windows of Mary's bedroom to escape. But gradually she settled in and even slept on the bed and soon over my feet.

Gradually, we expanded Mooshi's living space to half the bottom floor of the house and eventually she could roam through the entire house but always under supervision to avoid Nuppy attacks. After Nuppy's death, Mooshi became the queen of the house! She got to know Bogie, Fluffy, and George and got along with them fine.

In Montclair, Mooshi continued her habit of watching the world go by as she sat on the driveway from dusk until bedtime. All I had to do was to call her in for the night and she would run downstairs to sleep under my feet on the bed. Mooshi was used to seeing urban wildlife like raccoons and skunks. When Rocky the raccoon and her four offsprings made a habit of stopping by to eat leftover cat food and wash their paws in their water bowl, Mooshi liked to watch them.

In Sebastopol, Mooshi continued these habits except here I worried about coyotes that she was not familiar with. But she was very cautious and stayed close to home. Mooshi enjoyed the acreage and the rich rodent life that goes with it. She climbed trees and when the garden took shape she enjoyed taking naps there in the warmth of the sun.

Mooshi did not let me handle her. She only liked and allowed me and Mary to brush her. So to take Mooshi to a veterinarian appointment or to take her to Sebastopol, I had to place a laundry basket over her, slide a large flat cardboard under the laundry basket and tape the edges and then place this makeshift "carrying case" in the car. However, Mooshi was silent during such trips. Not all cats like to ride in a car.

Cats usually bond with what they consider their home. That was also true of Mooshi. But, over time, she bonded with me strongly enough that when I brought her to our new home on Darby Road, she acclimated within 48 hours!

When I let her inside the house, she began smelling the entire house. The next day, I left the sliding door open and Mooshi went outside. She started to smell the area around the house and then headed northeast towards the neighboring house. Afraid that she could get lost, I followed her with the basket and trapped her again and brought her back inside. I kept her in for a couple more days and then let her out. She had by then entirely accepted her new house and spent the first six months gopher hunting as Sebastopol is known as the gopher capital of the world, a cat's dreamland!

Soon after our arrival, I found the first feral cat colony on Darby Road and brought one of them, Sayda, home. Sayda was an older emotionally and physically scarred female. On Christmas 2011, I found a younger female tabby orange cat under the mailboxes by the creek on Darby Road and brought her home. Eventually Mooshi accepted both of them.

By March 2014, a large young muscular tomcat judged to be about two years old, who was dumped in the neighborhood a year earlier and had befriended me, finally came into the house. On a neighbor's suggestion, I called him Panther. Mooshi liked Panther but did not like his wild manner and Panther kept away from Mooshi's path. In April, 2015, I brought in Lulu who was the surviving member of the first Darby Road cat colony. In all this, it was clear that Mooshi remained the dominant cat. As Dr. Baldwin, who cared for Mooshi in the last three years of her life, wrote in a sympathy note: Mooshi "was a beautiful kitty with the soul of a lioness."

My relationship with Mooshi was based on total and unconditional love. I know that it was so from my side. But Mooshi, who was so protective of herself, also allowed herself to trust me from the beginning, and this trust grew over the thirteen years we knew each other. I like to think that she loved me like I loved her. I know this was true at least towards the end. But as soon as she had a chance to sleep in the same room as me she made sure to spend at least the last hour of the night laying on my legs. This habit gave me a bad back but it was well worth it.

As she became gradually disabled in the last year of her life, Mooshi let me take care of her daily needs including cleaning her butt and sometimes bathing her lower half in a bucket of warm cat-safe soapy water to ward off possible infections. When she was bedridden, I used to lean over her and kiss her face and body while rubbing her back and belly as she purred her heart out. Perhaps this was total and unconditional love on her part.

In 2012, Mooshi began to throw up clear liquid. Dr. Patricia Alexander initially diagnosed her with pancreatitis. But medication for pancreatitis did not seem to address her problem. Upon further consultations, Dr. Baldwin diagnosed her with irritable bowel disease (IBD) and prescribed prednisone. That seemed to do the trick. Mooshi felt better. But as I took her to her March 2012 appointment, the makeshift "carrying case" fell apart outside of the entrance to Analy Veterinary Hospital. Mooshi went loose in the parking lot. I might have been able to capture her but a staff member who came out to help instead scared Mooshi off into the yard of a neighboring house, which was beyond a wooden fence. When I went to the other side there was no sign of Mooshi and she was too scared and confused to respond to my calls. For the next seven days my life was entirely centered on attempts to find Mooshi. I have never lost a cat and did not know how a lost cat may behave. I got well intentioned advice though unfortunately, few were good advice. I spent my days from early in the morning to evening walking the neighborhood behind Analy Veterinary Hospital calling Mooshi's name. I posted a flier with her photo and offered a $100 reward to anyone with information leading to finding Mooshi. A psychic from Bodega Bay came to offer me advice and I was urged to phone another psychic who told me up front that she could see Mooshi in the cat heaven and I should simply make peace with her death and go home. Some people told me that Mooshi might walk all the way back to her house three miles away. I left the outside lights on and the cat door open at night hoping that Mooshi might return on her own. However, I was much more convinced by those who advised me that a lost frightened cat will simply find a hole and hide in a state of shock, that Mooshi was somewhere close to where she was lost. I knocked doors of all the houses behind the hospital and talked to anyone who opened the door and pleaded with them to keep an eye for Mooshi and to notify me immediately. On the sixth day, I had to visit my elderly parents in the East Bay when I learned someone in the neighborhood thought she had seen Mooshi. I was driving back home on Highway 101 and was stopped by highway patrol as I was driving at over 80 miles an hour. I got an expensive ticket. But as it turned out, it was worth it. On the woman's tip, that same day, which was a Sunday, I found Mooshi sitting quietly in a vacant lot near Analy Veterinary Hospital. I had her favorite food and offered her some. When she relaxed enough and began to eat her food, I trapped her but I could not open the car door while holding Mooshi's makeshift carrier. I did not want to lose her again. A man who had just come out of Taco Bell and was walking to his car was nearby. I pleaded with him to help me out with opening the car door for me. The nice man drove me and Mooshi to my house. Once there, I let Mooshi out inside the house. She immediately left for the outside. I offered her food and water and backed away. Mooshi ate her food and sometime later walked back into the house. The crisis was over.

However, after that horrible experience Mooshi's health declined. She was diagnosed with anemia and even worse Toxoplasmosis, a disease caused by the single celled parasite Toxoplasma gondii (T. gondii), which in last year of her life caused increasing paralysis in her back legs and lower body. She required multiple medications and in the last year she could not control her urine. I had to clean her bottom in lukewarm water with special soap and sometimes give her lower half a bath. Mooshi, who, together with

Nuppy, were the most independent-minded cats I have known, became entirely dependent on me.

In retrospect, I delayed euthanizing Mooshi perhaps by a year, as I could not stand the thought of losing her. She suffered from chronic kidney disease, the number one killer of older cats. As the kidneys fail, poison build up in the cat's body. Subcutaneous fluids are given to cats with kidney disease to flush out the poison from their bodies. Two days before her death, Mooshi refused to take subcutaneous fluids as it involved inserting a big needle under the skin of her back and the cat needs to stay put while the fluid emptied into her body from a plastic bag. The day before Mooshi's death the technician reported success in administering the fluids. But on the way home Mooshi tried to bite my hand as I was patting her back. She had never tried to bite me before. When I got home I found a bloody patch on her back. Mooshi had struggled while being forced to take the fluid. The same day, Dr. Baldwin reported the result of Mooshi's blood test. Her kidneys were failing fast. I had no choice but to accept losing her.

The Cats of
Darby Road, Sebastopol

Mooshi and I settled into a house on two acres of land
on Darby Road, outside Sebastopol, California, after my five-year unsuccessful quest, first to live in Cuba, and when that seemed impossible, in Costa Rica. There were different sets of reasons for each of these. But a common factor was the suffering of domesticated animals prevalent in those countries and elsewhere in Latin America (I have also seen it in Mexico and Venezuela). Once, in the charming small town of Trinidad, Cuba, I found a blind dog dying under the cocktail table I sat by to sip on a mojito and enjoy listening to live music. In Atenas, Costa Rica, dogs that were lucky to belong to someone spent their lives tied to a post on a short metal chain 24 hours a day—they are used as a burglary alarm. In Ensenada, Mexico, I saw that the dog in the house I stayed in had open wounds and that feral dogs laid dead by the side of the road, hit by cars.

Sebastopol, a town of some 8,000 people, seemed to offer some of the qualities of Vinales, Cuba, or Atenas, Costa Rica. My real estate agent, who cared for feral cats and rescued dogs, assured me that people in Sonoma County, especially in Sebastopol, were nice.

Darby Road, three miles southwest of Sebastopol, is a loop off Burnside Road, which snakes through the higher reaches of the area's hills. The house which I named La Casa de Los Gatos sits on two acres at the end of a cul-de-sac as a gate closes off the one-car lane to traffic. The house that faces northeast provides a private southeastern panoramic view of a gently sloping meadow that meet a dense growth of evergreens and deciduous trees that surround Atascadero Creek. A narrow band around the creek is public land and has been declared as a wildlife corridor. Thus, the location serves as refuge for wildlife, most notably deer and wild turkey, native and migratory hummingbirds, mourning doves, quails, and sparrows and finches. Crows and robins visit the area. There are, of course, raptors like red-tailed and red-shouldered hawks, barn and great horned owls, and, the sky is graced with floating turkey vultures. The Sebastopol area is known for its gopher and mole population and there are, of course, rats and mice, weasels and garter and gopher snakes, lizards, regional and migratory birds. Quail families live under densely grown blackberry bushes. There are small mammals like bobcats, raccoons, skunks, opossum, jack rabbits, and grey and red foxes. Larger predators like coyotes and mountain lions also go through the neighborhood. Although one could hear coyote calls at night and sometimes even see a lone coyote in daytime, mountain lions are rarely spotted.

Darby Road that slopes down from Burnside Road at about 15 degrees is surrounded by rows of apple and oak trees, and shrubs, mostly blackberries. A deep creek runs alongside its western side, which leads to Atascadero Creek. These creeks are active only during the rainy season and are dry the rest of the year.

About 1,000 feet to Atascadero Creek, Darby Road ends and a one lane paved private road that goes by La Casa de Los Gatos connects it to the eastern side of Darby Road that climbs up the hill to Burnside Road, completing a loop which people use, sometimes with their dog, to walk for pleasure or exercise. On this private lane where La Casa de Los Gatos is located there are only seven houses. The house is the last one on the lane just before the locked gate that makes Darby Road a cul-de-sac. There are houses on either side of Darby Road. Each set of houses has its own narrow private lane. A middle-age husband and wife own 150 acres of apple orchard and sell its harvest to the local apple cider industry. The orchard is run with help of a small crew of Mexican Americans, a few of whom are permanent and a few are seasonal. This is the only non-organic apple orchard in Sebastopol which used to be famous for its Gravenstein. But in recent decades growing grapes for the now world famous vineries of Napa and Sonoma counties has become a more lucrative option. There are two commercial vineyards on the eastern and southern sides of Darby Road.

My neighbors have cats and dogs, chicken and goats. There was also a rescued horse and a rescued donkey. In 2011, my next door neighbor had three ducks that she kept outdoors all the time. Within a few months, they were taken by coyotes.

One morning soon after I settled in my new residence, I was driving to town on the western side of Darby Road when I noticed two small orange cats running towards the car from the right hand side of the road. This portion of Darby Road is surrounded by the apple orchard with blackberry bushes and other bushes on both sides of the creek and blackberry bushes on the other side of the road that hide a neglected small house where a huge quiet man who works as a butcher at Costco lives. There is an open area on the creek side of the road that serves as the work area for the apple orchard where they place apple carts for loading and shipping at harvest time, which begins in midsummer and ends by winter. At the time, rusting disabled farm trucks and machinery, heaps of worn out tires and wasted wood made it clear that it was also a dumping ground. A few years later almost all of this mess was hauled away thanks to China's demand for scrap metals. The cats were coming from the location where a flatbed truck was half sunken into the ground and partially covered by blackberry bushes. There was also a rusting shell of an old truck 100 feet further on the same side of the road.

I pulled the car to the shoulder and stopped. When I stepped out, the cats came running to me rubbing their faces and sides against me. I immediately noticed that one of the orange cats had a large open wound above her right eye. They both looked very small, very thin. I thought they were kittens. I quickly figured out that they were starving cats. They wanted food.

I rushed back home and brought back several cans of cat food and a few dishes and a fork. It took them no time to swallow whatever I served. Meanwhile, I noticed that a black cat had also appeared, and in the distance, a calico cat. The black cat came closer and let me pat him.

I went back home to get more food.

Thus began my relationship with the feral cat colony on Darby Road. The first couple of weeks the cats devoured anything I gave them and licked dishes clean. They were very much undernourished and both orange kitties appeared seriously sick. The orange kitty with the wound over her right eye was by far the friendliest. She actually wanted me to pat her as much as she wanted to eat her food. The other orange kitty sounded as if she suffered from an upper-respiratory infection. She was skittish but being so starved she allowed me to touch her while she was eating. I was so busy with these two cats that the black cat and the calico cat simply ate their food at a distance.

After the immediate problem of severe malnutrition was alleviated and the cats began to simply eat their food as opposed to swallowing it as fast as they could, I decided to take the orange kitty with the open wound to a veterinarian. I thought that a raccoon or a fox, both of whom I saw when I was feeding the cats, might have bitten her and the wound was not healing due to bacterial infection. The raccoon and the fox were there in mid-day, an unusual time for them to be active. Apparently, someone had left unattended food for the cats and the raccoon and the fox had learned their routine and simply scared off the cats and ate the food, leaving the cats starving.

I borrowed a raccoon trap from Greg, my neighbor, and made an appointment (subject to being able to trap the cat) with Analy Veterinary Hospital, which is a fifteen-minutes drive from my home. On that Thursday morning I placed a small amount of food on a plate deep inside the trap, set the trap, and waited for the orange kitty with the wound to show up. She usually came first. However, the second orange kitty that usually did not show up early and sometimes not at all arrived and walked directly into the trap. I closed it manually and took the cat to the appointment.

We registered the cat as Orange Kitty Number One. The cat was very docile. Dr. Baldwin, who eventually became my go-to veterinarian and a friend, examined her. The tests for feline leukemia and feline immunodeficiency virus (FIV) were negative. She was given a dose of Convenia (cefovecin sodium), slow-release antibiotic, to treat her upper respiratory infection. I also learned that the cat was female and spayed and between 9 to 11 years old—an old age for a feral cat. Almost all her teeth and half her tongue were missing, probably due to a blow to the head either by an accident, such as being hit by a car, or by someone kicking her in the head. I learned later that she was also almost deaf. The notion that someone could have brutalized the cat is not far-fetched. As I noted earlier, George, in Montclair, was shot with a pellet gun.

I took the orange kitty home. I named her Sayda, a woman's name in Gilaki, a language spoken in the Caspian Sea region of Iran, and prepared the master bathroom and walk in closet for her.

The next day, I easily trapped the other orange cat. My neighbor who came to help feed the other cats while I took the cat to her appointment was amazed at how trusting this sweet cat was. We signed her in as Orange Kitty Number Two.

Dr. Baldwin almost immediately suggested that the wound that did not heal was probably advanced skin cancer. To examine her further, she had to use anesthesia. I left the cat with her and went home to sit by the phone. A call came in by mid-day. Dr. Baldwin told me that the cat was bleeding under anesthesia probably because she had eaten rodents with rat poison.

Rat poison is a potent anticoagulant—it kills rodents by causing severe internal bleeding. Rat poison is known to kill all kinds of animals up the food chain, including raptors, bobcats, and mountain lions. After a long period of activism "The California Ecosystems Protection Act" was passed in September 2020 that prohibits most uses of second-generation anticoagulant rodenticides.

Dr. Baldwin told me that she would do her best to save the cat. A little later she called to say that the bleeding had stopped but the wound was not operable and the cat seemed to be in late stages of skin cancer. She recommended that I give her permission to end her life while she was under anesthesia. Her suggestion was a rational choice—the cat probably would not have lived much longer and would have died a painful death. I fought back tears as I gave her "my consent" while thinking to myself: who am I to issue such a "consent?"

My neighbor, who knew about what was happening that morning, came to comfort me. I began to weep again. All the forgotten pains of my decision to euthanize Nuppy had reemerged. I felt the little kitty that was so sweet never had someone to take care of her and love her back. That is the tragedy of feral cats, bred to be loved by humans and denied this very same love.

VI. Sayda

Meanwhile, her sister, Sayda, vocalized her painful life as a feral cat. She cried when she used the box. She cried when she ate her food. And sometimes she cried in the middle of the night. That worried me. At the same time, she ate with gusto, a good sign of her desire to live and get stronger. She also began to enjoy some other comforts of living at home. Within a few days, she began sleeping in her doughnut-shaped bed.

To make sure she could sleep well I spent a number of hours each night sleeping with Sayda on the floor of the walk-in closet. This seemed to comfort Sayda as she sometimes curled up in my armpit or just above my head on the carpet and fell asleep. She also learned to enjoy being brushed—and she did need it as her fur formed into mats. Sayda's acceptance of my companionship was due to the small size of the closet and the bathroom to which she was confined. Each time I reached out to touch her, her initial reaction was to recoil. But once she was touched she relaxed and sometimes even purred softly.

I did not fully realize that a feral cat needs months to acclimate to her new home and bond with a human. So, I began to leave the bathroom door open so Sayda could walk into the large living room full of sunlight. Sayda did come to the door but would not cross into the living room. After a while, I brought her into the living rooms in my arms to sit by me on the sofa. This was fine as long as I sat by her. As soon as I moved to do something elsewhere in the house Sadya would run back to the closet. She did not feel safe in open spaces.

Meanwhile, Mooshi was curious about this new visitor. Whenever she tried to stick her head inside Sayda's turf she was hissed at and chased away by Sayda. As much as Sayda was docile towards humans she was aggressive towards other cats. Of course, she was bluffing given her small body and bone structure. I still do not understand how small cats sometimes bully large ones; female cats bully male cats, etc.

After a few weeks living in the walk-in closet and the master bathroom, Sayda discovered the loft. The shape of the loft follows the A-frame structure of the house. The ceiling slopes down on both sides making it very hard for a person to reach under it in both directions which in effect are "crawl spaces." The loft faces picture-frame windows with a beautiful view of the meadow and woodland on one side, and the northern garden and the narrow low traffic private road on the other, which everyone considers an extension of Darby Road.

One day, I could not find Sayda in her closet. As the bathroom door was always left open, I looked elsewhere in the house and found her in a dark corner of the attic. From that day on Sayda made the loft her turf. At night she ventured downstairs to use her box, which was still in the master bathroom. Once I realized Sayda was going to stay upstairs, I took her box to the attic so she did not need to come downstairs to use it.

Sayda spent the next couple of months hiding behind and under the bed in the loft or in its dark corners. I was no longer able to touch her or brush her. She would run away. I learned that she was putting up with me while in the closet as there was nowhere to hide!

One night, frustrated by Sayda's behavior, I laid on my belly on the carpet facing her under the bed and talked to her for about ten minutes. I asked her why she was playing this game. "Am I not the same person who held you, fed you, brushed you? Why are you now acting as if I am a threat?" I suggested she should afford herself more comfort. Why spend most of her time under the bed as opposed to elsewhere more comfortable in the loft? I then went downstairs to go to sleep for the night.

I do not know what might account for it, but the next day I found Sayda sitting in the loft by the bed and not under it. She never went back to sleeping or hiding under the bed!

A couple of months later I had a similar monologue with her, this time telling her that I lost my patience with her not ever coming downstairs. There is sunshine there and she could be in the company of Mooshi and Sunny (I will tell her story in a moment) and me.

The next day, Sayda came downstairs and sat on an Iranian cushion a couple of feet away from the workstation in my study. From then on, Sayda came downstairs every morning after her breakfast and remained there, catching the sunlight as late as mid-day. Sometimes she also came down at night to sit with the rest of us as I watched a movie or relaxed on the sofa listening to jazz with Sunny on my lap.

Sayda also ventured outside a few times. However, it was clear that she felt very unsafe because she was almost deaf and constantly surprised by people and animals showing up in her field of vision blurred by cataract.

For the first eight months Sayda's health seemed to fluctuate between poor to somewhat better. Her appetite was not great. She had formed a large mat on her back that obviously bothered her. She seemed unwell and showed obsessive/compulsive behavior by licking fur off behind both her back legs and by licking the carpet. She also exhibited behavior as if she was constipated or had a problem swallowing her food. One day, all of a sudden, she stopped eating. This went on for a few days.

One morning when she was sunbathing downstairs, I put a laundry basket over her, slipped a flattened book box under her and taped the basket over it securely. I took her to the veterinary hospital. Dr. Cloninger found no mass in Sayda's intestines, but she did find her to suffer from a blood infection common to feral cats. She gave her a Convenia injection and some medication to take by mouth. I put the pills in treat-like pill pockets and Sayda ate them.

Within a few days she felt better except for the onset of diarrhea. After ten days, I called Dr. Cloninger and she agreed to stop the antibiotics.

Sayda's appetite and behavior improved and she actually put on a little weight. Of course, she was still a very small cat.

Sayda lived in the house for three years. However, towards the end, her health deteriorated and she needed multiple medications she would not take. At the time she was perhaps twelve years old by Dr. Baldwin's estimate. That was a long life for a cat with disabilities and trauma of a hard life, all of which limited her abilities to enjoy the pleasures of everyday life. Sayda had nightmares and woke up crying loudly. Only when I rushed upstairs to talk to her did she calm down and perhaps fall asleep again.

In October, 2014 after a consultation with Dr. Baldwin, I decided that Sadya's suffering outweighed her rare pleasures of everyday life. What broke my heart was that on the day she was to be euthanized she came downstairs, went just outside of the sliding door, and sat on the door mat enjoying the warmth of the autumn sun. That was my only chance to grab her and take her to be euthanized.

I buried Sayda under the Japanese maple tree in the East Garden. I placed a large rock on her grave. I could do little to make Sayda happier. But at least, I tried to ease her pain.

VII. Smokey

After I took Sayda home and had her sister euthanized in September, 2011, two cats were left in the colony on Darby Road: the calico cat who I named Calico and the black cat who I named Lulu. A little after I had established a feeding routine for them, occasionally another cat showed up for food. He was a small grey-blue male cat that was not neutered, who had small ears, short hair, and was quick moving and pushy. He stayed away from me but he was not shy like Calico was. He tended to rush toward either Lulu or Calico while they were eating to push them away to eat from their bowl even when he had his own bowl of the same food.

When I inquired from neighbors about this cat, Jennie, an unusually robust woman in her eighties who was the co-owner of the houses on an eight-acre vineyard and lived in the smaller of two houses there, exclaimed: "Oh, this is Smokey!" She said Smokey had been around for many years (her estimate was eleven to thirteen years) and that her late husband used to feed him from time to time in the garage. Jennie still gave Smokey a saucer of milk on occasions. Obviously, they liked Smokey but never adopted him.

Smokey was a very intelligent cat. He used his front paws to move food around in his bowl to get at it better. Also, he did seem to have a sort of friendship with Lulu—the two greeted each other with what appeared to be a kiss. Still, Smokey had half-playful paw fights with Lulu and with Calico. Increasingly, Smokey showed up more often. By then with John's know-how and able assistance, a very tall and kind older neighbor, we had two cat condos built for Calico and Lulu as the nights were getting frosty. I asked John for help to built a third one for Smokey as well. Later, my other neighbor and friend, Greg, also a very capable builder, help me out by building a feeding station for rainy days which I placed in front of the cat condos John had built to give the cats more protection against coyotes (see, the front cover of the book for a photo).

In the next couple of months Smokey and I became close enough that he would do somersaults for me to draw my attention to pat and brush him. I bought a brush for Smokey as I already had a brush for Lulu. Gradually Smokey learned to like being brushed while eating from his bowl.

However, by December, I began noticing lumps on Smokey's face and infection in his eyes. Also, he needed to be neutered. After making an appointment for him at Analy Veterinary Hospital, I trapped Smokey on Martin Luther King's Day, Monday, January 17, 2012, and took him in.

It became a messy affair when the door to the trap failed and Smokey got out inside my Toyota Prius as I was driving him to his appointment. When we got there the staff had to sedate him to catch and take him to the examination room.

It turned out that poor Smokey had advanced FIV disease which lower immunity for opportunistic infections, several kinds of cancer, and blood diseases. The lumps in his face and his eye infections were the symptoms. Dr. Cloninger, who I spoke with on the phone, recommended euthanizing Smokey. I gave my consent.

Smokey could have been a wonderful companion for Jennie and her husband had they adopted him in his youth, neutered him, and taken care of him. He was highly intelligent and displayed affection towards me. He was friends with Lulu who showed signs of wondering about what had happened to Smokey. It took Lulu some time not to look for Smokey.

I had to take my car to a professional cleaners as Smokey had urinated in the car in his state of anxiety and fear. He had every right to fear his situation. There lies the quandary of humans who take up the task of managing non-human animals. To love a cat and to put him to sleep because he could be suffering otherwise or become a danger to other cats have caused me again and again to question domestication. We have been playing God with other species much more in line with the literal interpretation of Genesis than in accordance with the ethics based on the Darwinian evolutionary theory.

VIII. Calico

The local lore had it that Calico was an older matriarch who gave birth a number of times before she was spayed. No one knows where her kittens went. I have seen no sign of them in the neighborhood. Presumably they have all died or been taken. Calico was really a Calimanco or Clouded Tiger type of cat by her fur color. That is, her fur's basic color was black covered by spots and strips of lighter and darker orange. Calico was very protective of herself. Even Lulu could not get too close to her or there would have been a paw fight. Being an old cat, she spent a lot of time in her "den" and came out only for sunshine or fresh air or to hunt gophers and watch birds only when it was quiet in her neighborhood. She liked to go across the road to the rundown shed of the Costco butcher's house. Not being home often, his yard was overgrown with blackberries and other volunteers, a perfect place for feral cats and wildlife.

Given Calico's disposition, I never tried to trap her and take her to the veterinarian hospital. I reasoned that even if they found any aliments I could not medicate her. Thankfully, she held up well. There were periods, a day or two and rarely longer, when she did not show much appetite or did not even show up to eat. I knew she was not feeling well. But she bounced back each time and resumed her routine. Calico was not a big eater but she had more heft to her than Lulu. Although I could not give Calico anti-flea medication, I gave her deworming medication when I I dewormed Lulu. Cats can get parasites from rodents they eat or from fleas that feed on them.

When I arrived as usual at seven in the morning to serve breakfast to Calico and Lulu on April 13, 2015, there was no sign of either cat. It took three days before Lulu finally showed up, clearly still afraid. I had heard coyotes the previous nights roaming in the neighborhood. When I arrived in the neighborhood in August 2011 there were red foxes and grey foxes.

Then coyotes arrived and the foxes disappeared. Coyotes kill foxes. Some foxes moved into the residential neighborhoods of Sebastopol for safety. But feral cats bond with their place and will not move away. They have to do their best to hide from the hungry coyotes. Older cats who cannot hear or see well or cannot run fast can fall prey to coyotes. One day I found a coyote sniffing around the cat condos on Darby Road. He left when I arrived. Coyotes knew there were cats there. I had created all kinds of obstacles for larger-than-cat predators to be able to get to the cat condos and provided escape routes for Calico and Lulu. Still, it appeared to me that coyotes had surprised and taken Calico. Lulu must have seen the violent encounter that traumatized him. I had always wanted to take Lulu home. He loved human companionship and should have never been forced to be a feral cat. But I always reasoned it would be unfair to take Lulu home and leave Calico alone. Calico would hate being taken inside a house. So Lulu stayed a feral cat until Calico's demise. Three days later, I grabbed and put him in a carrier and took him home.

IX. Lulu

A beautiful black cat with shiny fur and yellow-green eyes and a touch of white in his chest, a long and thin body, and a lovable warm personality, Lulu must have been someone's cat dumped on Darby Road. He was the first of three male black cats I found dumped on Darby Road that I brought into the house. Sonoma County Humane Society gives material incentives to those who adopt black cats because of the prevalence of the superstition that black cats bring bad luck. Lulu absolutely loved human companionship and would easily bond with any friendly person. Yet, I was the only one who took a consistent interest in him. Everyday, I spent a fair amount of time brushing, holding, hugging, and kissing Lulu before , during and after he ate his meal (he took a break for love and then ate some more). He liked being brushed, to be picked up, and to sit on my lap as I squatted on the ground and being held in my arms as I stood up and walked around.

About a month after I found the cat colony, I trapped Lulu after a week of training him to eat inside the trap. He got so used to the trap that one morning I simply closed the trap door on him, covered the trap in a blanket so he would feel less stressed (cats prefer enclosed spaces when in stress) and took him to Analy Veterinary Hospital for an appointment I had already made. Dr. Baldwin examined Lulu and found him to be in generally good health on a physical exam and I took him home to wait for the lab results.

I had prepared the master bathroom with a carpeted walk-in closet for Lulu. Lulu hated his new space. No cat likes an unknown territory with strange smells and sounds. Displaying his anxiety, Lulu did not use his bedding and preferred to sleep on the drain in the bathtub. He hissed at me when I offered to brush him and did not eat well.

We had a typical spell of hot October weather. So, on Lulu's second day, I opened the window above the sink to let some fresh air inside.

The next morning, I found that Lulu was gone. He had pressed the window to the left, pushed the screen off and took off. I found Lulu waiting for me at his usual spot. He greeted me as if nothing had happened: sweet and wanting to be brushed. I served him his breakfast.

The next day, the antibody test for FIV came back positive. This sank my heart. But the false-positive rate for the antibody test is 25%. I asked for an ELISA test that actually looks for the FIV virus. That test came in negative. The only way for both tests to have been correct was for Lulu to have been infected within the past few months—the virus can still hide but the antibody can be present due to the body's defense system activity.

I decided not to pursue further testing for FIV infection because there is nothing one can do if a cat is in fact infected but to take as good care of him as possible. Also, Lulu was not an aggressive cat and even if he was FIV positive there was very little chance of him biting another cat to pass on the virus.

Three years later, Lulu was doing well. What worried me though was that he ate a lot but did not gain any weight. He also developed an eye infection. I trapped Lulu again and took him to Dr. Baldwin. She prescribed a drop for the eye infection but she also determined Lulu suffered from hyperthyroidism, caused by an increase in production of thyroid hormones (known as T3 and T4) from an enlarged thyroid gland in the neck.

I had to give Lulu pills twice daily, which he took wrapped in a pill pocket. But after a while, he knew about the pill, which he did not like. It became something of a struggle.

By that time, Calico had died and Lulu was brought inside the house. I kept him in my bedroom and master bathroom for four month and he broke out four times, each time going back to his old spot. Finally, I had to replace the window screens with a cat-proof variety. He gradually accepted the house and got along even with Panther who, at first, was not accepting of Lulu. In September 2015, after consultation with Dr. Baldwin and making an appointment for Lulu on a waiting list, I took Lulu to University of California at Davis's Small Animal Clinic 75 miles away for radioactive iodine therapy, which is considered the treatment of choice for cats with hyperthyroidism. The treatment would require quarantining the cat for three weeks after the treatment including collecting and disposing of his urine and feces properly as all are radioactive for up to three weeks.

To do the procedure, they had to run a series of tests on Lulu. The preliminary tests showed an abnormality in Lulu's gut. They asked me for permission to do exploratory surgery which I did not realize that it involved cutting open his belly to take samples of his intestine. I had no choice but to accept. We returned for a second time and I had to leave Lulu overnight for the surgery. The results showed Lulu was suffering from large cell lymphoma which usually kills a cat in a short period of time unless chemotherapy is used to extend the life of the cat by a few months.

After consulting with an oncologist and Dr. Baldwin, I decided to put Lulu on palliative care instead of on any chemotherapy regimens. Lulu's lymphoma was aggressive and chemotherapy would not have added but a few months more to his life and surely would have caused him much discomfort with many hospital visits.

While it is possible to explain to a human cancer patient why enduring chemotherapy may be a good option to extend life even for a short time and let the patient decide whether the hardship is worth accepting, the same is not true for a cat.

Lulu lived about three months after the diagnosis. He was on prednisone (a steroid) to maintain his appetite. In the last couple of weeks I painfully was witness to his day by day decline. He was as sweet as always, loved to be close to me, especially by sitting on my head, his favorite spot. He spent time in the garden enjoying sun light. Beginning February

11, Lulu showed no more interest in food. He looked terrible, his body shrunken and his eyes looking sick. On Friday night and in the early hours of Saturday, Lulu was clearly uncomfortable. He laid down next to me on the bed in the loft but was unable to sleep. In the wee hours of Saturday morning, I decided to take him to VCA Animal Hospital in Rohnert Park, a thirty minute drive, which is always open, to be euthanized. I called them and took Lulu there. As always, Lulu was quiet in the car.

It was about 5:50 Saturday morning before dawn, February 13, that they handed to me the carrier with Lulu's lifeless body inside.

When I walked out it was still dark and there was nobody else in the huge parking lot. Tears rolled down my face as I felt the weight of his body —I felt defeated and lonely. Death is an amazing life event. It is final. There is no return. What was real becomes imaginary.

As I drove home on the almost empty highway 116, my few years of companionship with Lulu went through my mind as if on a movie screen.

I buried Lulu in a grave under the redwood trees. This was significant in more than one way. All the time I knew Lulu, I always wished him to come home with me. I did not take him in because I did not want Calico to become a lonely older feral cat on Darby Road. But, at long last, Lulu came home to live with me. He had become part of the household.

X. Sunny

On Christmas morning, 2011, I saw a very small orange cat running under the blackberry bushes when I stopped to pick up my copy of the New York Times from the mailbox. On Darby Road, because houses are far apart, mailboxes of all houses on a private road are installed at the corner where the two roads meet. My mailbox is about 900 feet away from the house. Often I take my mail as I drive home.

The next morning as I was returning from serving breakfast to Lulu and Calico, I saw the orange kitty again and called her. She stopped just under the first row of blackberry bushes. I opened a can of cat food and put it in a bowl near her. She quickly walked to the bowl and started eating. In no time, she ate all that I had dished out for her. I gave her the rest of the can and it was gone in no time. Meanwhile, I realized she did not mind me getting closer to serve more food. I began gently rubbing her back while she ate. She ate three 6 oz. cans of food before she was satisfied. Then she walked under the bushes and disappeared.

The next day, she was there waiting for me. I had a new cat to feed on Darby Road. The difference was that this little cat was totally friendly and apparently unattached to a hole she would call her home. I could pick her up and she would just purr. After a few days, I decided to take her home. I picked her up and began walking towards home. Halfway to the house, she became nervous and wanted to jump down. Her body stiffened and her claws sank into my chest. I realized I could not take her home simply by carrying her in my arms.

The next day, I brought a cardboard box and tried to place her inside it to take her home. She wiggled out of it after I carried her some distance.

I decided to trap her and it was easily done on the first try. I took her for a visit with Dr. Baldwin. She was found to be healthy, about two years old with a hernia due to a poor spaying operation. Dr. Baldwin thought it was not a serious condition.

I called her Sunny after the name Mike and Emily, two of my neighbors, renters at the marijuana farm near the Atascadero Creek, had given to the sister of Sayda that I had to have euthanized. (As I learned later, it was Mike and Emily who were throwing food for the feral colony cats causing raccoons and foxes to show up for food just before I first started taking care of Calico and Lulu).

Sunny did look like she could be the offspring of either of the two tabby orange kitty sisters. Some time later, I saw another tabby orange cat on Burnside Road who appeared feral and looked like Sunny. I saw her from time to time until about the time Sunny died. They could have been siblings.

Sunny spent the first night in the master bathroom. I remember she defecated in the bed I gave her and slept inside the litter box! The second night she was out in the living room sitting on my lap as I watched a movie. The transition was amazingly fast.

Still, knowing there were other cats in the house, she was cautious, spending most of her time behind the bookshelves. She was tiny enough to fit. Gradually, she began to sit on the shelves. Her favorite was the philosophy section.

Sunny began to put on weight and get stronger and more comfortable in the house. In her first six months she almost grew to twice her starvation weight.

Sunny's demeanor helped her stay out of trouble. She was happy to be at the bottom of the pack and would lie on her back on the ground when challenged by Mooshi, who wanted to show who was the boss. That explained why she was so deprived of food. She was outcompeted by other cats and went hungry for a long time. Also, it explained why she was not bitten by FIV infected cats—she did not contest anyone. Still, as I learned later, Sunny turned out to be a great mouser. She was patient, fast and had formidable claws. She patiently sat by a gopher or mole hole for hours to let her prey come close enough and then she would pounce! I saw her eating numerous rodents but unfortunately also a few birds as well.

Mooshi did not like Sunny at the beginning. It took a year before she accepted her in the bedroom and soon after, both cats shared the bed with me.

For the first four months Sunny had her routine. In the morning, she would leave the house for a day under blackberry bushes on the opposite side of the Plumfield Academy dormitory which houses a few teenage boys under the short term jurisdiction of Sonoma County. Every evening I had to go bring Sunny back home. She wanted me to catch her and bring her back home in my arms so she made it easy for me to catch her. Some days, as we walked back home, Oliver, the neighbor's dog on the opposite side of the road, barked at us from across the fence and Sunny sank her claws into my chest. Eventually, Sunny left and returned home on her own accord. Still, for another year, each time someone came to the house for a visit, Sunny took refuge outside. She eventually realized that home was the safest place to be. Once that was established, Sunny stayed inside even when roofers put a new roof over the house, making a lot of noise in the process!

Friday nights is my time off to relax on the sofa listing to jazz or to watch a movie. Sunny liked to lay on my belly or legs facing away from me when I stretched out on the sofa or sat on my lap when I watched a movie. I often felt a deep sense of gratitude for finding such a wonderful companion from behind the blackberry bushes!

I lost Sunny on Thanksgiving Day, November 23, 2017. The following is my tribute to her written at the time.

I am tempted to find ways
to say that "I love you"
but Nature has already
said them all.

Let us then surrender,
all together,
to the bright beaches
and the rugged mountain tops.

Let us lay in leaf beds
and meadows of tender
new grasses courting
delicately budding flowers.

From "Simply Divine," Jaime K. Reaser, *Scared Reciprocity: Courting Beloved in Everyday Life*, 2012.

Sunny suffered from chronic kidney disease and lung cancer. The night before her death she had trouble breathing, probably due to the spread of her lung cancer. She was euthanized at about 9:30 in the morning while resting on my lap at VCA Animal Hospital.

Sunny's troubles surfaced on the day before Christmas 2016, when she stopped eating. Her veterinarian tried everything in the book to find out why but could not. Finally, a barium X-ray showed a possible obstruction in her stomach. Sunny was referred to the best surgeon in the area who suggested "exploratory surgery." That meant opening up Sunny's underside with a long incision to examine the inside of her GI tract and take biopsies for pathological examination. The only thing they found was "moderate irritable bowel disease" (IBD), a form of allergy to food protein in various meats the cat eats. Of course, one does not need such an invasive surgery to diagnose IBD. The IBD diagnosis seemed to explain Sunny's refusal to eat her old favorites and her lack of appetite. To recover from the surgery, Sunny was fitted with a feeding tube, which I used to give her liquid food, water, and medication for a month. Sunny was now on a lifelong daily dose of prednisolone to control her IBD.

In June, Sunny was found to suffer from moderate chronic kidney disease, the number one cause of feline mortality. Prognosis for Sunny changed from a chronic but manageable IBD to terminal chronic kidney disease. Typically, a cat with such a condition is placed on a special "kidney-friendly" diet and supplements to help flush out toxins from her body. But Sunny was a finicky eater and would not eat a "kidney-friendly" diet. And, the supplements I had to shove down her throat twice daily gave her a bad case of diarrhea. So, we settled for any food she would eat and stopped giving her the supplements. Thus, her prognosis became more dire. Still, finding food that Sunny liked and getting her to eat "just a bit more" became a constant concern of mine. And, she gradually ate less and less even of things she did like, except for rodents and birds.

In September, an X-ray taken for another purpose showed a dark spot in her lungs. The radiologist confirmed a rare lung cancer that afflicts mostly female cats. Sunny was now cornered by two terminal diseases. In late October, Dr. Baldwin found a mass in Sunny's mammary glands. Whether this was new cancer or metastasis of her lung cancer we did not know and had no practical value for her care. It was merely another sign that Sunny's life was about to end.

Sunny was receiving subcutaneous fluids four times a week, something like dialysis for cats, for which we made trips to her veterinarian hospital. Meanwhile, Sunny had lost more than 3.5 lb. since June. With about 6.5 lb. of weight, she was skin and bones. Still, Sunny ventured outside, enjoyed the garden, and hunted. A week before her demise, I found her munching on a field mouse under the rosemary bushes.

Dr. Baldwin had warned me that if she began having problem breathing, it would be time to let her go. The night before Thanksgiving, at about 9 p.m Sunny, who was laying on my lap, began choking. In reaction, she jumped off the bed and returned to the closet where she had camped the past few days and nights. Her eyes looked terrified and she seemed sick and in pain. I tried to calm her down by giving her a dose of pain medication. She slept in the closet the rest of the night.

Thanksgiving Day morning, I took Sunny to the VCA Animal Center. Very caring and sensitive staff attended to Sunny and me. The technician and the veterinarian who examined and treated Sunny had tears in their eyes when they were caring for Sunny. Their examination room looked more like a cozy living room with a loveseat. I sat on the sofa and placed Sunny on my lap on a soft blanket. She seemed comfortable and resigned. After examining Sunny, the veterinarian concurred that it was time to let Sunny go. Sunny was given pain medication and within ten minutes she was relaxed and sleepy. Then, her right forearm was fitted with a catheter. After once again asking for my agreement, the veterinarian gave Sunny another dose of strong pain medication through the catheter that relaxed her completely. The veterinarian again asked for my permission and then injected Sunny through the catheter with the medication that stopped her heart. Sunny gave a slight sigh and I was left alone to pick up the pieces of my broken heart.

Sunny was a gentle, feminine soul who often felt at ease sitting in the garden in a warm spot or "watching" a movie with me at night or being in my company anytime. Perhaps because of this strong bond of friendship between us I miss her very much. There is a constant gap in my daily life. I miss her gentle personality, her devotion, and the warmth of her body close to mine. There is a world of difference between watching a movie and watching a movie with Sunny on my lap.

My beloved Sunny, you will be in my heart and mind for as long as I live.

The Second Feral Cat Colony on Darby Road

In late July 2011, when I first spotted the house I live in now after a seven-month search, I visited it with my real estate agent on a sunny afternoon. As she and I sat down to discuss strategy on how to approach the seller, a small old man walking with a cane and accompanied by an old dog arrived. He introduced himself as Stuart, a neighbor, and sat down with us for a welcome conversation. I was eager to learn about the neighborhood and he was happy to talk about it.

Stuart owned the first house on the road next to the creek. It was a small long-neglected white house with no landscaping. Across the unpaved driveway was a huge rundown structure that years ago served as a small chicken farm. The tin roof of this large structure was mostly gone and piles of junk were left there to rot. There were also pallets loaded with rocks of various kinds. I later learned that Stuart was a rock collector.

After I moved in I met a tall middle-age man named Steven who walked Stuart's old dog. It turned out that Stuart was in the process of relocating to Colorado and Steven was caring for his dog and two cats and the house while Stuart was away to Colorado.

Steven had lived in Sonoma County for a long time and had a small business, which he lost to a massive heart attack that also took away all his savings. He was too incapacitated to work and was supported partially by a small disability pension. As it turned out, Stuart himself was gravely ill with pancreatic cancer.

Despite this, Stuart was hell bent on relocating to Colorado and to move his belongings in his truck and trailer himself. On his last trip, he took his large rock collection. I never saw Stuart again as he died not long after he settled in his new home in Colorado.

Stuart had two wonderful young male cats: Ernie who was black and white and Frank who was black. Both had great personalities. Neither was neutered. Ernie roamed the neighborhood fighting with other male cats and the permanent scar near the right side of Panther's nose is probably from a fight with Ernie. At the time, Panther, who eventually came to live with me, was dumped in the neighborhood at age one! He was not neutered either.

Ernie used to visit the house and hang out with Mooshi, who seemed to like him. One day, Katherine, the neighbor who owned the acreage where the Darby Road cat colony I was taking care of lived, called me highly agitated. She complained that a big black and

white cat had been fighting with her renter's cat and wanted me to stop him from visiting her "property." When I told her the cat's description matched Ernie and that Ernie was not a feral cat and belonged to Stuart, she responded that she would shoot Ernie next time he made trouble!

I called Steven and pleaded with him to get Stuart's permission to neuter Ernie and Frank. I even suggested that I would pay for the veterinarian visit. Fortunately, Stuart gave his permission and also paid for the procedure.

Frank was also an amazing cat. Unlike Ernie, Frank stayed close to home. One could see him laying down in the driveway. Frank also loved dogs. When my friends and neighbors, Les and Nancy, walked their large black dog Elko, Frank would walk up to Elko and sniff him. Luckily, Elko was a gentle giant! Les and Nancy had rescued Elko from a small caged area he was placed in by the original owner of the apple orchard who wanted a dog but was unwilling to spend any time with him. On Les and Nancy's diplomatic pleading, he released Elko to their care of and they gave Elko the best care any dog would ever want. He lived a long and happy life and I socialized with him many times.

After Stuart died, a woman who was taking care of his estate came from Colorado and took Ernie and Frank.

While living in Stuart's house, Steven had brought in a small male Siamese cat named Coco who was FIV positive and as Steven was preparing to move away, Coco seemed gravely ill with very badly infected eyes. Steven could not afford veterinary care for Coco or even high-quality cat food that could have boosted his immune system. Luckily, Les and Nancy adopted Coco. They took Coco for veterinarian care, gave him high quality food, a comfortable home, and a lot of love. Coco revived, his eyes cleared up, his fur became fuller and shiny, and he enjoyed games Nancy and Les played with him. He lived a couple of years longer in happiness.

XI. Oskar

Steven was also feeding Oskar, a smokey-colored small male feral cat with a square face and a great, dignified and mellow personality. Unbeknownst to Stuart, Oskar had made the basement of his house into his den and could get in and out through a window with broken glass. Steven served Oskar's food by the doorsteps of the house or in the rundown chicken barn. Steven told me that Oskar sometimes came inside the house and slept near him with Coco.

Before Stuart died, Steven found low-income housing in Salinas, Monterey County. He asked me if I would take care of Oskar. I accepted. Steven left in July 2012 and I began to serve Oskar food and water in the chicken barn. Soon, however, Stuart placed another man as the house sitter while he was looking for a buyer. While this new house sitter, Dick, was also a low-income middle age white man, unlike Steven who was among the more intellectually inclined of my neighbors, he was a hoodlum. Soon after he arrived, Dick told me I could not serve Oskar's meals in the chicken farm that offered the cat protection from rain. I was forced to serve Oskar's food across the street under the blackberry bushes. This put Oskar and me in danger of incoming cars as the location was at the ninety-degree corner on Darby Road. There was no other location with relative protection from rain. Still unhappy about me serving Oskar across the road from the house, Dick tried to run me over three times in the course of a couple of months when I was crossing the road to serve Oskar or stand by his spot to tend to his needs. I was forced to report these incidents to the County Sheriff and two of my neighbors. Dick's unprovoked hostile actions stopped only after, at my request, Steven reported them to Stuart in Colorado who ordered him to stop. Stuart knew that he would be responsible for Dick's action while house sitting on his behalf. Luckily, a young couple bought the house and Dick had to leave. By then Oskar was used to his new spot and I continued to care for him there.

But Oskar was an old cat. He obviously was dragged down by his age and possible illness. By late 2014, Oskar had sores on his ear, which reminded me of the orange kitty's skin cancer. I was debating whether to trap Oskar and have him euthanized or let him die of his illness in due course. Oskar ate with great appetite and was a regular. One evening in March 2015, Oskar showed up and ate well and left to sleep in his den under the house. I never saw him again.

Oskar had a dignified personality, was well mannered towards other cats, and allowed me to get close to him but I could not touch him. In summertime he liked me to serve his dinner in the apple orchard under the blackberry bushes on the edge of the creek. This required me to walk on the dusty ground making my shoes and pants dirty. But I complied with his wishes and sat nearby talking to him. Oskar would have been a great friend and companion for any caring human being whom he never found.

XII. Mocha

When I was still serving Oskar in the old chicken farm, a large male Siamese cat appeared who was so hungry that he stole Oskar's food as I was looking elsewhere. Soon, I began to serve the cat whom I named Mocha as well, except he was very skittish and would not approach his food dish unless I had backed off a fair distance. When Mocha made a cavity under a pile of pallets at the far corner of the old chicken farm his home, I began serving him food and water there. Unbeknownst to me, Mocha was gravely ill and within a few months stopped eating and then disappeared the way dying feral cats often do.

XIII. Latte, Echo, and Max

Some time after I began serving meals to Oskar across Darby Road under the blackberry bushes, a younger female Siamese cat appeared inside the dry creek from the direction of the marijuana farm. The marijuana farm operated under the radar by a husband and wife team, Joe and Jane, who employed a few occasional workers, sometimes of shady character. The farm was an open secret in the neighborhood, but I think the old timers in the neighborhood were quiet about it because it had replaced an infamous methamphetamine lab that was busted.

Joe and Jane rented a small structure there to various tenants. The result was two families of feral cats. One family of cats was Siamese. A young "enterprising" couple decided to breed Siamese cats and sell them. When nobody bought the kittens and their monetary situation deteriorated, they left the farm and the cats to fend off for themselves. Another family of cats lived under the barn at the farm. These poor cats had to deal with four marijuana dogs kept by Joe and Jane. Marijuana growers keep dogs to ward off thieves who may raid the farm for its expensive crop or even for stash of cash sometimes kept on the farm. These dogs are trained to bark and bite.

While one family of cats took refuge under the barn in the farm, the Siamese cats were driven off the farm. I met three of them. I have already talked about Coco and Mocha as well as the female Siamese cat I saw in the dry creek. I suspect that Mocha was probably the father of these cats.

The female Siamese cat that showed up in the creek eventually came to Oskar's feeding place under the blackberry bushes. I named her Latte, a beautiful female cat who was very skittish but also very hungry. It took her a few weeks before hunger forced her to join Oskar and eat from the bowl I left for her. Clearly, she and Oskar knew each other as neither cat minded the other. In fact, Oskar and Latte became friends as both cats had very sweet personalities.

On the day before Valentine's Day 2015, a short while before Oskar died, I saw Latte sitting next to him after their dinner under the blackberry bushes, putting a front leg around his back and licking his face. To me, that was a clear case of affection, as Latte seemed to comfort Oskar. She probably sensed his predicament.

After Oskar died, Latte was my only feral cat on Darby Road. I began to debate if I should try to take her home, a process that would be especially hard on her as she remained skittish.

Mike and Emily, an Irish-American couple in their forties who were renters at the marijuana farm for years decided to move to a larger apartment in town as Mike, who worked at Whole Foods at a low-level managerial job, got a raise. For years, they were taking care of a family of feral cats who lived under the barn in the farm. For a few months after their move, they made a point of coming to feed these cats outside the gate of the marijuana farm some hundred yards from where I served food to Latte. Unlike me, they did not follow an exact schedule so they fed only cats that showed up. The cats that missed a meal were on their own. I also noticed they did not wash the dishes in which they served food and water to the cats. That could have made the cats sick.

After a while, I did not see Mike or Emily anymore. I assumed they came at a time that I was not on the road taking care of Latte. One day, two small smokey and white-colored cats appeared under the big oak tree across from where I served food to Latte. The fur on their back looked odd—the fur seemed burned in spots on the back of one cat and as stripes on the back of the other cat. They were very hungry and I served them food. They began to show up again and soon were regulars. I called them Spots and Stripes. Later, it occurred to me that the cats might have been burned by electric fences around the marijuana farm.

I never saw Mike and Emily on Darby Road again.

One day when I was shopping at Whole Foods, I ran into Mike. He seemed embarrassed to see me. He blurted out something like: "We thought since you are taking care of Latte you would not mind taking care of our cats… it was not practical for us to come to Darby Road every day."

To be sure, the round trip from their home in town to where they fed the cats was about 20 minutes. But nobody serves feral cats for its convenience. While Mike was a full-time worker, Emily was not working. Once the cats were no longer outside their front door, Mile and Emily decided they were too much of a burden and decided to dump them on me.

When I settled in the house on Darby Road, I invited neighbors over for dinner to get to know one another. I invited Mike and Emily after I met them while serving the cats in the original feral cat colony. We shared a love for the feral cats. Mike who had studied music in college was an aspiring lead guitarist in a local hard rock band. Playing the guitar was his main interest in life. Emily was an aspiring writer. I knew they had modest means and I invited them out to dinner a couple of times to socialize. I counted them as newly found friends. I was entirely taken aback when they dumped an entire family of feral cats on me. How they could do this without asking me was beyond my comprehension. There were other options available to them. Some of these cats were entirely friendly and could have been taken to the Humane Society for adoption. In fact, I had suggested this to Mike and had offered to help out.

At Whole Foods, Mike said they took home with them the large, aggressive male in the marijuana farm feral cat family. But Mike never told me how many cats they left behind. Soon, I found a miserable old cat with half of her face and one eye eaten by skin cancer who showed up hungry for food. I learned that this was the mother cat. I had to trap and take her to be euthanized, a heart-wrenching experience.

Spots and Stripes lost their spots and stripes in a few months. I learned that they were brother and sister and that Mike and Emily had named the sister Echo because her paws were white on smokey-colored legs. Both were very sweet cats, but the male cat stopped coming by and I learned that he was found dead in the farm apparently without any signs of injury. Later, when I found the skull of a bobcat under the redwood tree at La Casa de Los Gatos, a biologist friend of mine hypothesized it was probably due to rat poisoning. Some vineyards around Darby Road may be still using rodenticides to control the rat population. There is a campaign to urge vineyards to install barn owl boxes, which offer a natural method for rodent control.

A little later, another very small male cat came. Mike and Emily had named him Max. Max was mischievous. While Echo respected Latte's privacy and did not venture into her eating spot, Max would not. I had to make sure that he did not raid Latte's food while she was eating. Max was the smallest of the three cats. So, his behavior was simply annoying to them but did not cause them any serious trouble.

Latte was punctual and consistent—she never missed a meal unless she was sick or when it was really stormy with heavy rainfall that filled the creek with rushing water four feet high. Echo and Max were not consistent or punctual. Echo hated the rain and would never show up on a rainy day. When it rained for three days she did not come to eat for three days! I had a feeling that they either successfully hunted rodents in the barn where they lived or people on the farm threw some food at them. But Joe and Jane who owned the farm neither liked the cats nor liked me to take care of them. Jane who was always at the farm and walked her four dogs without leashes, in particular, had some feeling of animosity towards me. Early on I found the water bowl I left for the cats each morning was missing. I found it in the creek. Someone had tossed it there. Jane's hostility resulted in one of her dogs attacking me and biting my leg for which I had to call my doctor and get a rabies shot. Neither Jane nor Joe ever apologized. I had to report the incident to Animal Control of Sonoma County. But I refused to press charges against Jane. Animal Control sent someone to talk to Jane and Joe and the dog was quarantined for a period of time. Jane and Joe were ordered to use leashes when they walked their dogs.

The cats, often Echo but sometimes Max, got sick from time to time and would not show up for an extended period. Echo held the record of not showing up for as long as two weeks and when she returned she was skin and bones. Each time I feared for her life and each time she surprised me by bouncing back and regaining her lost weight by eating a lot. In most cases, it is futile to trap a feral cat for a veterinarian visit because it is not possible to medicate them. Still, I dewormed them from time to time using pill pockets. Once, when I was trying to apply anti-flea medication to Latte she almost clawed my fingers.

On the evening of the day before Thanksgiving 2017, Max came for dinner. He was not eating well for a few weeks and did not eat much that evening. I never saw Max after that evening. Like Mocha and Oskar, Max simply disappeared.

In the last year of their lives, I got closer to Echo and Latte. Echo loved to be brushed and I brushed her twice a day sometimes. Latte, who now allowed me to pat her and enjoyed it, learned from Echo's example and allowed me, reluctantly, to brush her as well.

Alas, their health deteriorated in 2018. It was through my urging that they ate a fair amount at each meal. When Echo stopped eating, I would move her dish close to where Latte ate and she ate some more. When Latte quit eating early, I knew rubbing her forehead and chin would encourage her to eat more.

Before the Kincade Fire in Sonoma County, which burned October 23 to November 6, 2019, both cats ate very little. Latte exhibited a worrisome panting as her lower abdomen pulsed uncontrollably. I had been wondering earlier why she ate so well but was so skinny. I feared cancer was eating her from the inside. But I did not know why she was panting. Just before the wildfire started, Echo also did not eat much and a few times she threw up and that seemed to have become a pattern. She also drank water frequently. I feared renal failure.

In the early hours of Sunday, October 25, large sections of western Sonoma County, which included our neighborhood, were ordered to evacuate at four in the morning. I was only able to put Siah in a carrier and left for San Rafael to stay with friends. Panther had gone out an hour before the evacuation order and was not responding to my calls. Of course, I had no hope of taking Echo and Latte.

The evacuation order was issued because of high winds. The power company, PG&E, had cut off power to millions of residents. Tens of thousands were on the road trying to find a safe haven somewhere.

By early morning on Monday, the high winds had largely died down. I decided to return even though the evacuation order was not yet suspended. I made it back to Darby Road by about 8:30 a.m. There were only a few cars on the highway and even fewer on the country roads and none in the town. The air was filled with smoke.

When I got a tray of food and went to the road and called for Latte and Echo, Latte came out of the blackberry bushes with a loud heart-wrenching cry as if in sharp pain. Her abdomen was pulsing and despite my urging, she ate almost nothing. Echo came and ate a little but threw up her food; her saliva was sticky and foamy. She proceeded to try to drink some water.

I decided it was to time euthanize Latte—she seemed in pain, unable to eat, and was showing up because she wanted to see me or repeat an experience that was once rewarding to her. Analy Veterinarian Hospital was closed. But the VCA Hospital in Rohnert Park about 30 minutes away was open. I called them but there were 51 patients in line at that time. That was not a good time to take in Latte. The next morning, I called before I went to the road. There was only one patient in line.

When I called Latte, she came out of the blackberry bushes crying loudly, her abdomen pulsing rapidly. I offered her some food but she was not interested. She looked miserable as if about to die. I picked her up and wrapped her in a towel I had brought and placed her into a small carrier I had borrowed. She wiggled a moment in resistance. But then she became quiet, resting inside the carrier, wrapped in the towel.

As I drove to the VCA Animal Hospital I talked to Latte to give her some comfort. But I heard no response from her. I feared she was dead. I did not dare to look.

At VCA Animal Hospital, which was very quiet, I was taken into an examination room to wait for the attending veterinarian. It was Wednesday, October 28, at about 8:30 in the morning. A nurse came and took the carrier to another room. About ten minutes later, the attending veterinarian came into the room with a saddened face. He said: "I am sorry but Latte is already dead." Apparently, Latte who always feared people but learned to trust me had died of a heart attack as I tried to take her to be euthanized. I was relieved that she did not endure the torment of being taken to the hospital and being handled by people she did not know only to be euthanized.

On Sunday morning November 30 I took Echo to be euthanized. Her situation was different from Latte's in that she was not facing an immediate threat to her life like a failing heart. But she was weakened by not being able to hold down the food she ate and faced wasting away due to malnutrition. I was able to pick up Echo and place her inside that the carrier, closing the door on her. But she began to complain about her confinement as we drove the distance to the VCA Animal Hospital. A very intelligent cat, Echo did not seem like a good candidate to be euthanized. The middle-age woman who was the attending veterinarian wished to examine her before deciding that it was ethically the right course of action. Echo would not allow a proper examination and jumped out of the carrier and tried to jump up on the computer desk but could not. Her mere movement and apparent weakness convinced the veterinarian that she was an old cat and there was no way to walk her back to health. Given her condition as a feral cat, it was prudent to save her from the agony of dying from starvation that may take a few weeks. A crew came in to catch Echo and they took her to be euthanized. I declined the offer to be present. I did not have the courage to face it. She died at about 10:30, always a feisty, friendly, and beautiful cat.

I buried Latte and Echo below the redwood trees where Mooshi, Lulu, and Sunny were already buried. My neighbor and friend, Greg who had recently helped me with building a feeding station for Latte and Echo, used his tractor to bring a 160 lbs. rock on which Echo sat to view the vineyard and I brought the lighter flat rock where I had their water bowl placed for them. They serve as Echo's and Latte's tombstones.

XIV. Panther

In the summer of 2013, I began noticing a black cat traveling back and forth along the fence facing the Atascadero creek. I thought it might be a neighbor's cat. Soon, I noticed the cat approaching the house and spraying on the sidings of the house at each corner. He was scent marking.

I offered him food, which he gladly ate. He was a young black cat with a patch of white on his chest.

The young couple who bought Stuart's house had a relative in her thirties staying there for a few months while they did the preliminary work for rebuilding a new house on the foundation of the old. She and I talked as I took care of Oskar and Latte. It was she who suggested that the new cat looked like a black panther. I liked the name and called this new cat Panther.

Panther was obviously dumped in the neighborhood. Feral cats whom I have taken care of on Darby Road all had their own "home" and lived close to it. A cat that wanders the neighborhood is a cat that does not yet have a place to call home. As cats are territorial, a dumped cat is pushed out by other animals that live there, domesticated or wild. A dumped cat is scared, hungry, and gets into fights with cats who already have their own turf. That is why Panther was wandering about the neighborhood and that is how he got a big cut on his nose that has left a permanent scar.

In March 2014, I trapped Panther and took him to Dr. Baldwin. He was FIV positive. He was given rabies and other immunization shots and neutered. I kept Panther in the small bathroom for three weeks. He was a nice cat but a vocalizer. One day when I was going to East Bay to see my elderly parents and let Panther roam free in the house, he learned about the cat door and took off.

For three months, I hardly ever saw Panther. Suddenly in long summer evenings, he began a strange routine of running through the open sliding door by the sofa into the house to the steps leading to the loft as I sat on the sofa with Sunny on my lap and Mooshi resting on the Iranian rug nearby. After some time in the loft, he would run downstairs to eat from the bowls of cat food I keep on the living room floor. And then, he would take off running out through the same open sliding door. Gradually, Panther stayed inside for increasingly longer time. One evening, when he ran inside the house I simply closed off the doors for the night and he stayed with the rest of us in the house. He became part of the family.

Panther stayed away from Mooshi but as he learned how docile Sunny was he chased her in the garden from time to time. I had to put a stop to his aggressive behavior by calling on him to stop and he by and large left Sunny alone. When Lulu arrived in the house there was a short period of adjustment with Panther. They paw-fought a couple of times but I stopped that and they soon did not mind each other.

Panther has become the longest term cat resident of La Casa de Los Gatos. He has also fully developed his habits. He prefers the outdoors especially at night even when it is biting cold. I am resigned to his routine of nagging me at wee hours of the night to go out and then getting up once or a few times some time later to let him back inside the house. When he was younger Panther would stay out for hours, worrying me given that coyotes are sometimes in the neighborhood. More recently, he simply goes out to sit on the door mat to watch the night life in the neighborhood as cats, like owls and deer, have great night vision. Aside from Sayda who was also a vocalizer, Panther is the only cat I have known who is vocal. He is also the only cat I know that routinely scent mark his turf, as dogs do. Panther loves sunbathing and demands to be brushed each morning. He loves to play even though he is now a middle age cat. One of my joys is to take a siesta with Panther on the sofa who sleeps in his bed on his back with legs high stretched in four directions. Panther has largely accepted Siah as the top cat. But thankfully, he sometimes pushes back against Siah who likes to dominate Panther and me both. Of course, it is now mostly posturing. But from time to time there is a brief fight and I have to take whoever gets bitten to Dr. Baldwin for treatment of a puncture. While such fighting between Panther and Siah was more frequent in the first two years after Siah came in, it is a rare occurrence now. Most cats family species, including big cats, are solitary animals. We humans domesticated house cats to be with us and force some to live together in a small space we call home. Such conflicts among them are really our making. Recently, Panther has built up enough confidence to come to my bed where Siah has monopolized and three of us sleep close to each other. Those nights, although I feel crammed by two big cats next to me on a queen-size bed, I sleep better.

XV. Siah

In the fall of 2017, when I was serving Latte and Echo on
Darby Road, I spotted a square-shaped muscular male black cat that walked alongside Darby road towards us. The cat would not stop even though cat food was being served but continue on towards the marijuana farm. I had never seen this cat before and it was most likely a "feral" cat as he was not neutered. What was strange about this cat was that he showed no interest in food or the cats I was serving and in the initial contact allowed me to rub his back gently. He then continued walking as if he was heading to a specific destination. For some time, I feared he was a new cat from the marijuana farm. If Joe and Jane wanted to have cats they could have taken care of Echo and Max and their siblings, I reasoned. Latte, Echo, and Max seemed at ease with him being around. He did not come by frequently or with any regularity.

A couple of months later one afternoon as I worked in the garden, I spotted the black cat on the Western garden of the house. He had found where I lived. Panther also spotted the black cat and immediately chased after him and he ran away. Over the next few weeks, the black cat came by more frequently and he and Panther began to fight which I had to stop. By August 2017, the black cat whom I named Siah ("black" in Farsi) began laying atop a relatively flat rock in the succulent garden by the steps leading to the house. I began to serve him food, which he ate with gusto. Panther took notice of this and he sat on the opposite side of the steps on the top of the concrete retaining wall. Panther was determined to drive Siah away and Siah was determined to camp by the house! I saw no other way but to bring him in. So I left the house door ajar and began serving food to him increasingly closer to the door to the house. Siah began to come closer to the house. After eating his meal, Siah would return to his spot on the rock. Each evening before dark when I had to close the door, I asked him if he wanted to come in. He would remain seated atop the rock on a towel I put there to make it softer for him. Sometime after I closed the door, Siah would leave. I did not know where he would go. I feared for him because of the coyotes that were active in the neighborhood. Did he have a safe spot for the night?

Finally, by October, Siah began to come inside to eat his food. I left the door open to let him know he could leave if he wanted. Meanwhile, I made an appointment for him at Pet Care East in Santa Rosa that is open 24 hours everyday of the year. I borrowed Greg's trap and began acclimating Siah to eat inside of it. On the evening of October 20, 2018, I trapped Siah and took him to Pet Care East. He stayed overnight and the next day he was neutered and vaccinated. Siah was also diagnosed as FIV positive.

Like Panther and Lulu, Siah was dumped perhaps because he is black. Like Panther, he spotted La Casa de Los Gatos as his best option and picked me as his butler. He showed me affection during our "getting to know each other" period in the garden. I would sit on the edge of the concrete retaining wall with my back to Siah. He would then come close to rub his face against my arm, scent marking me as his own. Once or twice he bit my bare arm hard enough to draw blood. As I learned later, Siah has an oral fixation like Nuppy did. This was as much their way of asserting their domination as a sign of affection as biting gradually became gentler. Siah kept biting me until about a year ago when he mostly stopped. He sometimes licks me like all cats do as a sign of affection.

Siah likes to visit the garden during the day and ventures outside when it gets dark. He has a routine as follows: at nightfall he wants me to open the front door so he can venture outside. Some time later, he comes in through the cat door to eat some food. He then wants me to open the front door for him again so he can go through this routine once more. Depending on how he feels, he may repeat this a few times before settling inside for the night. Siah is probably the most "intelligent" of all the cats I have ever known. I have a cat fountain and a bowl of water that I refresh each morning. Panther drinks from the fountain but Siah prefers the bowl. When the water is not fresh, he sits by the bowl waiting for me to freshen up the water before he drinks. He has trained me to give him can food by jumping up on the dryer in the utility room where cat food is also stored. He sits there until I serve him what he wants.

Siah follows me around like a dog when I work in the garden or to leave leftover cat food for Vennie, the turkey vulture who shows up most evenings for a snack. Both Panther and Siah like to follow me when I go to the yoga room to exercise. Both cats want me to "tuck them in" when it is time for them to take a nap or sleep for the night. Panther likes to follow me down the road to our neighbor's barn and pasture for two goats, Heidi and Brownie, to give them treats of organic bananas and organic corn chips. Sometimes, Siah follows us although he does not like to venture off from the house especially going on the road. Unlike Panther, Siah does not especially like being brushed but loves to get a massage something Panther has also learned to like. Siah nibbles on my ankle as I stand up working on the computer to get my attention that he like yet another massage! So I end up massaging both cats a number of times each day. Unlike Panther, Siah does not talk except on rare occasions when he get really excited.

In brief, together with Panther and Siah we have formed a family enjoying our days at La Casa de Los Gatos.

Cats in
Historical Perspective

The reader may wonder why hundreds of millions of cats are feral in all corners of the world and somehow humanity seems unable or uninterested in doing anything to resolve this tragic situation. As I have detailed with the stories of 20 feral cats, feral cats have a miserable life unless someone intervenes to help them, in the best case to give them a loving home. Yet, most people are either ignorant of the plight of feral cats or contribute to their misery by dumping cats they do not want and refusing to spay and neuter cats. I hope I have also underscored that once these cats are given a loving home, their lives improves and their personalities develop to varying degrees depending on their individual situations. As domesticated animals, cats need human companionship.

Scientists have traced back the house cat to the Fertile Crescent, a crescent-shaped region in the Middle East, spanning modern day Iraq, Syria, Lebanon, Palestine, Egypt together with southeastern Turkey and western Iran (some include Cyprus). It is one of the regions in the world where farming settlements first emerged. It is sometimes called the Cradle of Civilization because of the rise of Sumer in Mesopotamia 5,000 years ago ,which is generally accepted as the first civilization.

According to a 2017 study by Claudio Ottoni and her colleagues, cat domestication took place in two strains, but all domestic cats have a common ancestor: the North African / Southwest Asian wildcat, *Felis silvestris lybica* . By studying ancient cat DNA from all over the world, the researchers found that cat domestication began in the Fertile Crescent in the Neolithic period and accelerated later in ancient Egypt in the Classical period. After systematic farming of wheat, barley, millet, and emmer got under way in the Fertile Crescent, rodents and birds were attracted to the fields and silos. They were followed by wildcats. Of the nearly 40 wildcat species at the time, a smaller wildcat with a genetic variance that allowed it to become friendly with people gradually became semi-domesticated.

It took thousands of years for subsistence farmers to produce a sustained agricultural surplus. But once that happened, social differentiation followed, resulting in private property, patriarchy, and the State. Early city-states like Uruk, gradually linked up with one another, creating the early civilizations, like Sumer.

Thus, domestication of the cat followed the rise of agriculture around 10,000 years ago. Domestication is the process of domination and control of species in which the domesticated species becomes dependent on humans for its reproduction as a species. Scientists have shown that domestication has changed not only the domesticated species but also humans, the domesticator.

There was a paradigmatic shift in human relations with the rest of nature as agriculture and herding require domestication which has been the pillar of all civilization in the past 5,000 years. As hunter-gatherers, anatomically modern humans (Homo sapiens) who emerged at least 300,000 years ago had viewed themselves as a tiny part of the rest of the world which they saw was alive with many personages, animate and inanimate, who they saw as kin. Agriculture changed all that in favor of a human-centered view of the world (anthropocentrism), which gives moral standing to humans over the rest of nature, and views nonhuman nature as "natural resource" for human purpose. Thus, the ethical dilemma I cited by quoting Singer's *Animal Liberation* about the principle of equal consideration.

Thus, the cat spread across the world through migration of people. With the rise of the capitalist civilization, breeding of dogs became fashionable in England. Soon, cat breeding followed and cats and dogs became "pets" among the more affluent social groups. Keeping cats indoors all the time was not possible—nor was it even a goal—until several important 20th century innovations: refrigeration, kitty litter, and the development veterinarian science to provide spaying and neutering of cats and dogs. Still, most cats have never been spayed or neutered, resulting in a continued increase of feral cat groups all over the world. Being a formidable predator, the explosive population of cats has become an ecological problem. In the United States alone, cats kill an average of over 2 billion birds and 12 billion mammals each year. Cats are the leading cause of non-natural bird deaths, accounting for just under 75%, according to a 2015 study.

As it turns out, the crisis of feral cats worldwide is part of the much larger crisis of the anthropocentric civilization, which in its latest stage, the industrial capitalist civilization, has created existential crises for humanity such as catastrophic climate change, the Sixth Extinction, mounting pandemics, and nuclear holocaust. To resolve the problem of feral cats, we must transcend anthropocentric industrial capitalist civilization in the direction of a much smaller human population that will produce and consume differently and in much smaller quantity using technologies that would not harm species and ecosystems. The new human society will abandon domestication and subordination of other species for human purpose. As Henry David Thoreau put it: "In wildness is the salvation of the world."

Photo Gallery

The house on Chelton Drive, Montclair, Oakland

NUPPY (Fall of 1992 – May 15, 2008)

GEORGE (birthdate unknown – Spring 2009)

George in the background sitting in the street with
Fluffy in front of him and Bogie on the top step.

CAPTION: Gravely ill, George on the day before he went
away to die in isolation. Bogie is standing above him.

FLUFFY (birthdate unknown – December 23, 2016)

BOGIE (1994 – February 26, 2015)

Rocky who visited with her babies for leftover food

Survey Research Center, University of California, Berkeley

Mooshi spent the first six years of her life
living in spaces under this building.
(Photo credit: Wikimedia Commons)

MOOSHI (2000 – November 4, 2016)

Mooshi watching from the balcony of the Survey
Research Center as employees leaving for the day

La Casa de Los Gatos, Sebastopol, California

CALICO (birthdate unknown – April 13, 2015)

SMOKEY (birthdate unknown – January 17, 2012)

Calico and Lulu eating their dinner in front of their newly built feeding station on Darby Road.

SAYDA (birthdate unknown – October 12, 2014)

LULU (birthdate unknown – February 13, 2016)

OSKAR (birthdate unknown – March 2015)

Oskar with Latte when she started getting served with him under the blackberry bushes.

SUNNY (birthdate unknown – November 23, 2017)

When I first saw Sunny, she suffered from malnutrition and was tiny.

MAX (Birthdate unknown – After Thanksgiving Day, November 22, 2018)

LATTE (birthdate unknown – October 30, 2019)

ECHO (birthdate unknown – November 3, 2019)

PANTHER (Estimated birthdate 2012)

The young Panther in 2013 as he decided to
claim La Casa de Los Gatos as his own.

THE CAT MAN OF DARBY ROAD

Panther likes climbing up to the roof of the tool shed.

Panther loves his siesta often next to me on the sofa

SIAH (estimated birthdate 2015)

Panther and Siah in a rare moment of mutual serenity.